A CRAFTER'S BOOK OF
SANTAS

A CRAFTER'S BOOK OF
SANTAS

More Than 50 Festive Projects

Leslie Dierks

Sterling Publishing Co., Inc.   New York
A STERLING/LARK BOOK

ART DIRECTOR: **Chris Bryant**
PHOTOGRAPHY: **Evan Bracken**
ILLUSTRATIONS: **Kay Holmes Stafford**
PRODUCTION: **Chris Bryant**

Library of Congress Cataloging-in-Publication Data

Dierks, Leslie.
    A crafter's book of Santas : more than fifty festive projects / Leslie Dierks.
       p.   cm.
    "A Sterling/Lark book."
    Includes index.
    ISBN 0-8069-8164-4
    1. Christmas decorations.   2. Santa Claus in art.   I. Title.
TT900.C4D54   1996
745.594'12—dc20
                        96-1185
                        CIP

10 9 8 7 6 5 4 3 2 1

A Sterling/Lark Book

Published by Sterling Publishing Company, Inc.
387 Park Avenue South, New York, NY 10016

Created and produced by Altamont Press, Inc.
50 College Street, Asheville, NC 28801

© 1996, Altamont Press

Distributed in Canada by Sterling Publishing,
c/o Canadian Manda Group, One Atlantic Avenue, Suite 105, Toronto, Ontario, Canada M6K 3E7

Distributed in Great Britain and Europe by Cassell PLC,
Wellington House, 125 Strand, London, England WC2R 0BB

Distributed in Australia by Capricorn Link (Australia) Pty Ltd.,
P.O. Box 6651, Baulkham Hills, Business Centre, NSW, Australia 2153

Printed and Bound in U.S.A.

ISBN 0-8069-8164-4

CONTENTS

INTRODUCTION

ALICE LAWSON LOOKS FORWARD TO THE DAY WHEN SHE CAN RETIRE AND CARVE SANTAS ON A FULL-TIME BASIS. THESE ARE A FEW SHE HAS KEPT FOR HERSELF; ALL THE OTHERS HAVE BEEN GIVEN TO FAMILY AND FRIENDS.

Of all the folk heroes who have been admired over the years, none has remained so steadfastly popular as the mythical being called Santa Claus. His appeal is easy to understand, for who could resist someone who is always full of good cheer and who always arrives bearing gifts?

Artists and crafters are especially fond of Santa because the wealth of tradition surrounding him allows them plenty of room for expressing their ideas. They can portray him as a saintly figure in the Old World style, as a humorous elf with magical qualities, or as a grandfatherly figure who loves all the world's children. For many, one Santa leads to another, and before long that fondness becomes a passion.

No matter if you're an all-time admirer of Santa Claus or simply looking for an out-of-the-ordinary gift to make for a friend or relative, you're certain to find many treats in the pages that follow. They're filled with Santas of every style and demeanor, from a dour Victorian to an enthusiastic golfer. Not all are three-dimensional figures; you'll also find sweaters, place mats, Christmas tree ornaments, and even a sampler with a Santa motif.

There are 52 projects in all—one for every week of the year—and they range from simple to complex. Many are perfect for beginners, but others assume some experience with the underlying technique, such as needlepoint, papier-mâché, or sewing. If you find a Santa you want to make but are unfamiliar with the medium, don't be discouraged. Simply consult one of the many basic how-to books in that craft, and return to your Santa after you feel more comfortable.

THE MAKING OF A LEGEND

Everyone knows Santa Claus; he's that plump jolly fellow in the red suit who bounces little children on his lap at the local department store. Or is he? Santa Claus, a.k.a. St. Nicholas, Kris Kringle, and Father Christmas, has appeared in many forms over the years. Some have described him as a cleric in the robe and miter of a bishop. Others have seen him as a stooped, lean, elderly figure in a hooded cloak. He's also been portrayed as a small, chubby elf dressed in a fur suit.

The story of Santa Claus began with a man named Nicholas, who was the Bishop of Myra in Asia Minor (now Turkey) during the fourth century A.D. Throughout his life, Nicholas was renowned for his generosity and kindness, especially to children, but it was after his death that the legends grew and he was canonized as a saint.

According to folklore, Saint Nicholas often went out at night to bring gifts to the needy, and he is often credited with performing miracles. One of the most commonly told stories relates how he restored the lives of three young boys who had been gruesomely murdered, and there are many tales of his sudden appearance in the midst of great storms to calm the sea and save floundering ships.

As his popularity and stature spread throughout Europe, Saint Nicholas became the patron saint of children, sailors, and the entire nation of Russia. December 6, the day of his death, became an official church holiday, and throughout medieval Europe this day brought great merrymaking and the exchange of gifts in his name.

The Protestant Reformation, which denounced the worship of saints, was responsible for moving the day of celebration to December 25 and for starting Santa Claus down the road of secularization. In countries with large Protestant populations, Christmas Day became the occasion for feasting, and the gift-bringer took on new personas. German traditions embraced at least four Christmas figures, including *Pelznickel* (Nicholas in furs), who brought treats for the good children, and his assistant *Knecht Ruprecht*, who carried a stick for whipping bad children. There were also *Weihnachtsmann*, a thin, stooped, and bearded old man who delivered his sackful of presents on Christmas Eve, and *Christkindl*, an ethereal, angelic character who represented the infant Christ.

9385 *Joyeux Noël*

Groeten van St. Nicolaas.

◀ IN FRANCE A SLENDER AND SERIOUS-LOOKING PÈRE NOËL (FATHER CHRISTMAS) BRINGS GIFTS TO THE CHILDREN.
Courtesy of Terry Taylor.

▲ IN THIS HAND-TINTED BLACK AND WHITE IMAGE, DUTCH CHILDREN LINE UP TO BE REWARDED—OR ADMONISHED—BY SAINT NICHOLAS.
Courtesy of Fred Kahn.

Съ Рождествомъ Христовымъ

◀ ALTHOUGH HE IS SHOWN HERE IN SECULAR DRESS, RUSSIA'S PATRON SAINT BRINGS CHRISTMAS GREETINGS AND PRESENTS TO THE CHILDREN.
Courtesy of Fred Kahn.

IN THIS DUTCH POSTCARD, *SINTER KLAAS* ARRIVES ON FOOT TO DELIVER PRESENTS TO THE TOWN'S CHILDREN.

Courtesy of Fred Kahn.

The most dramatic transformation of the saint took place in America during the 19th century. The Dutch immigrants, who settled in New Amsterdam (now New York), had brought with them their tradition of celebrating St. Nicholas Day and the nick-name *Sinter Klaas* for their favorite saint. These practices might have remained within that community—and we might not have the Santa we know today—had Washington Irving not written the book *Knickerbocker's History of New York*. Published in 1809, it was an amusing account of Dutch colonial life that included many references to Saint Nicholas. To add spice to his tale, Irving described the goodly saint not as a cleric but as a plump, jovial fellow who smoked a Dutchman's clay pipe and rode over rooftops, dropping presents down chimneys.

THIS GERMAN ▶ POSTCARD FROM THE EARLY 1900s IS LABELED KNECHT RUPRECHT, BUT SINCE HE IS CARRYING A BAG BRIMMING WITH TOYS AND NOT JUST A STICK, THE FIGURE IS MORE LIKELY WEIHNACHTSMAN.

Courtesy of Fred Kahn.

◀ "CAUGHT!" BY THOMAS NAST. THIS DRAWING SHOWS A PLUMP, FUR-CLAD SANTA WHO SMOKES A DUTCHMAN'S CLAY PIPE.

Several years later, a professor of biblical studies, Clement Clarke Moore, wrote what was destined to become the most popular of all Christmas stories—a poem entitled "An Account of a Visit from St. Nicholas." It begins "'T was the night before Christmas," and goes on to describe St. Nick as "a right jolly old elf" who arrives on the rooftop in a sleigh pulled by eight tiny reindeer. He enters via the chimney and is quick to fill the stockings with toys. When he exits back up the chimney and off to his next destination, it is with a magical flourish.

What Moore established in words, Thomas Nast confirmed—and embellished upon—in images. Nast was a political cartoonist who began working for *Harper's Illustrated Weekly* shortly before the start of the Civil War. In addition to his more serious drawings, he did an annual series of images of Santa. To these he brought many of the elaborate Christmas traditions of his native Bavaria, as well as the influence of Clement Moore's poem.

Included in his drawings were the embellishments we now take for granted at Christmastime, such as holly and mistletoe, and some of his images reinforced the notion that Santa rewarded good children and punished bad ones. Thomas Nast originated the concept that Santa Claus lives at the North Pole, and he was the first to show Santa in his workshop, making the toys he delivered.

IN THESE DRAWINGS, THOMAS NAST SHOWS HOW A ▶ RECENT INVENTION—THE TELEPHONE—MIGHT BE USED TO COMMUNICATE WITH SANTA AT THE NORTH POLE

"Hello! Santa Claus!'   "Hello! Little One!'

A THREE-STORY SANTA ▶ WELCOMES VISITORS TO SHELTON, WASHINGTON, WHICH IS NICKNAMED "CHRISTMASTOWN" BECAUSE OF ITS LARGE ANNUAL PRODUCTION OF CHRISTMAS TREES.
Courtesy of Terry Taylor.

Follow the Road Signs to Santa Claus Land, Santa Claus, Indiana

◀ IN SOME STATES, ENTIRE TOWNS HAVE BEEN NAMED IN HONOR OF SANTA CLAUS.
Courtesy of Terry Taylor.

YEAR-ROUND CHRISTMAS SHOPS ARE NOW COMMON THROUGHOUT THE AMERICAN LANDSCAPE.
Courtesy of Terry Taylor.
▼

Santa's popularity has continued to grow throughout the 20th century. During the 1930s he was adopted by the Coca-Cola Company as their product spokesman during the holiday season. Their advertising campaign, which ran prominently in popular magazines, on billboards, and at soda fountains, crystallized the current image of Santa. Here we saw for the first time the bright red suit, broad black belt, and shiny boots.

As America grew more prosperous in the years following World War II, Santa Villages and Christmas shops sprang up all over the country. Most are open all year round, and they continue to serve an audience that never tires of the joys of the Christmas season and the magic of Santa Claus.

 **SANTA STAR PILLOW**

Santa has the starring role in this holiday pillow designed by Vicki Gadberry. It's a perfect weekend project for using up some of your accumulated fabric scraps, and the piecework is simple enough even for beginning sewers.

MATERIALS & TOOLS

- scrap pieces of holiday fabrics
- scraps of white and black felt
- paper-backed fusible web (optional)
- sewing thread
- sewing machine
- iron
- fabric paints
- fabric glue
- 14" (35.6-cm) square pillow form
- stain-resisting spray

DECK THE HALLS

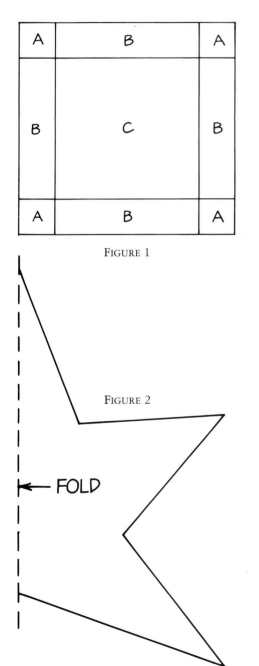

FIGURE 1

FIGURE 2

◄— FOLD

INSTRUCTIONS

1. Cut the fabric pieces as indicated in *figure 1*; the two D pieces overlap on the back to make the pillow cover function as a sham.

2. Enlarge the star pattern to fit the finished size of the center panel, piece C. Cut the star to size if you plan to attach it with fusible web. If you plan to sew the star to the pillow cover, add a seam allowance of ¼" (6 mm) all around. Attach the star to the center panel using your preferred method. Turn under and press the seam allowance before stitching.

3. Create the embellishments you desire for your Santa. In this pillow, an egg-shaped piece of white felt is used for Santa's hair and beard, and small pieces of black felt are made into boots and a belt. Cut a hole in the hair/beard to reveal a face painted onto a scrap of white cotton. His suspenders, hat, and bag are all made from holiday prints. Glue the embellishments in place, allowing each to dry before adding the next.

4. If desired, use a puff-type fabric paint to add fur trim to Santa's hat and suit.

5. Assemble the pieces of the front of the pillow in strips, creating two A/B/A pieces and one B/C/B segment. Now join the A/B/A pieces to the B/C/B piece. Sew all of the pieces together using a ½" (1.3-cm) seam.

6. Hem both D pieces for the back. Along one 16" (40.6-cm) edge of each piece, fold under ½" (1.3 cm) and press. Fold under another 1" (2.5 cm), press, and sew.

7. With right sides together, pin the front panel to both D pieces. The two D pieces should overlap. Sew a ½" (1.3-cm) seam on all four edges and trim the corners.

8. Turn the pillow cover right side out, pushing the corners into points. Press; then insert the pillow form. If desired, apply a stain—resisting spray to the pillow cover.

PIECE	QUANTITY	CUT SIZE	FINISHED SIZE
A	4	3" x 3" (7.6 x 7.6 CM)	2" x 2" (5.1 x 5.1 CM)
B	4	3" x 12" (7.6 x 30.5 CM)	2" x 11" (5.1 x 27.9 CM)
C	1	12" x 12" (30.5 x 30.5 CM)	11" x 11" (27.9 x 27.9 CM)
D	2	16" x 12" (40.6 x 30.5 CM)	15" x 10" (38.1 x 25.4 CM)

NEEDLEPOINT ORNAMENTS

Noted for her use of bright colors and attention to detail, needlepoint designer Catherine Reurs added a touch of whimsy to this trio of Santas. These are quick, fun projects to frame individually, hang together on a wide ribbon, or display as Christmas tree ornaments.

MATERIALS & TOOLS

- clear plastic needlepoint canvas (14 mesh)
- china marker, grease pencil, or felt pen
- #22 tapestry needle
- Paternayan Persian Tapestry Wool:

SANTA SAILING
3 yds. (2.7 m) white #260
2 yds. (1.8 m) red #970
2 yds. (1.8 m) green #680
1 yd. (91.4 cm) black #221
2 yds. (1.8 m) cobalt blue #540
1 yd. (91.4 cm) flesh #490
5 yds. (4.6 m) sky blue #544
1 yd. (91.4 cm) very pale blue #546
10 yds. (9.1 m) metallic gold

SANTA & FRIENDS
4 yds. (3.7 m) white #260
3 yds. (2.7 m) red #970
2 yds. (1.8 m) green #680
1 yd. (91.4 cm) black #221
1 yd. (91.4 cm) cobalt blue #540
1 yd. (91.4 cm) flesh #490
1 yd. (91.4 cm) very pale blue #546
2 yds. (1.8 m) golden brown #720
5 yds. (4.6 m) deep yellow #771
5 yds. (4.6 m) metallic gold
10 yds. (9.1 m) metallic red
10 yds. (9.1 m) metallic green

SANTA AT THE PYRAMIDS
1 yd. (91.4 cm) white #260
2 yds. (1.8 m) red #970
3 yds. (2.7 m) green #680
1 yd. (91.4 cm) black #221
1 yd. (91.4 cm) cobalt blue #540
1 yd. (91.4 cm) flesh #490
6 yds. (5.5 m) golden brown #720
5 yds. (4.6 m) yellow #772

DESIGN: CATHERINE REURS
SIZES: 3½" (8.9 CM) SQUARE AND 4" (10.2 CM) SQUARE

5 yds. (4.6 m) light purple #341
6 yds. (5.5 m) deep purple #340
10 yds. (9.1 m) metallic red
3 yds. (2.7 m) metallic silver

Instructions begin on page 14

SANTA SAILING

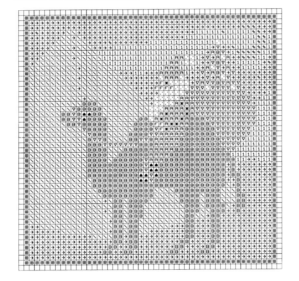

SANTA AT THE PYRAMIDS

SANTA & FRIENDS

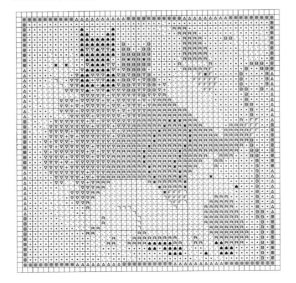

KEY TO CHARTS

	Color	Paternayan Wool
♠	= Black	#221
◥	= Metallic Silver	Silver
⌐	= Very Pale Blue	#546
∴	= White	#260
B	= Golden Brown	#720
+	= Metallic Gold	Gold
\	= Yellow	#772
o	= Dark Yellow	#771
✳	= Cobalt Blue	#540
/	= Sky Blue	#544
→	= Deep Purple	#340
1	= Light Purple	#341
F	= Flesh	#490
R	= Red	#970
⊞	= Metallic Red	Red
▽	= Green	#680
△	= Metallic Green	Green

Needlepoint Ornaments, continued

INSTRUCTIONS

1 ▪ Copy the pattern shape onto the plastic canvas before you cut the canvas to size. Mark the outline of each piece on the canvas and count the bars in each piece to check it before cutting. When cutting the canvas, cut the space between the bars and trim off all the plastic nubs. Then clean off the outline marks.

2 ▪ Separate the 3-ply yarn into single plies and thread the needle with one ply of yarn. Work all of the designs with a single ply.

3 ▪ Referring to the charts, work the designs in the continental or basketweave stitch, starting in the center or in one corner. Stitch the design details first; then fill in the background. Finish with the outside border.

4 ▪ Needlepoint hints: Wherever possible, work the lightest colors first. This prevents you from catching any dark threads and stitching them into the lighter colors. Don't pull the stitches too tightly, or the canvas may tear. When you come to the end of a strand of wool, gently run it through the back of 7 to 10 stitches to prevent it from working loose. Don't carry the wool from one area of color to another of the same color unless it is within five to six stitches in any direction. Leave the outside row on all sides unstitched until the rest of the piece is complete; then use a binding stitch to finish the edges.

5 ▪ Because the plastic canvas is rigid, your finished needlepoint won't need to be blocked. For ornaments, sew a ribbon loop on the back of each design and glue felt or ultrasuede on the back to finish it. To make a small wall hanging, slip stitch or glue each Santa to a wide ribbon, leaving 2" (5.1 cm) of ribbon showing between each. Add a simple bow at the top. Alternatively, frame each Santa individually and display the trio on your mantelpiece.

SANTA STOCKING

Lori Kerr's proficiency in appliqué and machine embroidery are clearly demonstrated in her design of this Christmas stocking. Whether packed full of treats or standing ready for the big event on Christmas eve, this jolly fellow will bring a smile to all who behold him.

MATERIALS & TOOLS

- ¾ yd. (68.6 cm) cap fabric
- ¾ yd. (68.6 cm) lining
- ⅛ yd. (11.4 cm) cap band fabric
- ¼ yd. (22.9 cm) face fabric
- ½ yd. (45.7 cm) beard fabric
- ⅛ yd (11.4 cm) contrasting beard fabric
- fabric scraps in various colors
- tracing wheel and paper or iron-on transfer pen
- paper-backed fusible web
- iron
- fusible tear-away interfacing
- rayon machine embroidery thread
- sewing machine
- pink colored pencil

INSTRUCTIONS

1 ▪ After placing the cap, tab, and face/beard patterns (*fig. 1*) on the appropriate fabrics, cut two pieces of each. Cut two pieces of the cap and face/beard patterns from the lining fabric.

2 ▪ Trace all of the facial features onto the face fabric.

3 ▪ Before the appliqué pieces are traced onto the paper-backed fusible webbing, all of the patterns must be reversed.

This can be done by holding the designs up to a sunny window and tracing them onto the back of the paper. Fuse the web to the motif fabrics; then trace the reversed designs onto the backing. Remember to extend the edges of all the underlying pieces so the fabrics will overlap slightly.

4 ▪ Cut the designs from the bonded fabric, peel off the backing, and position them as desired (see *figure 2*). Allow the cap band to overextend the cap slightly so that you can fuse it to the face after all the other features have been placed and pressed. When you're satisfied with the placement of the motifs, press them at the recommended iron setting.

5 ▪ Press fusible tear-away interfacing onto the back of the entire stocking front and to the portion of the back that includes the cap band to stabilize the machine stitching.

6 ▪ Stitch the appliqué using your choice of stitches; those shown here are satin stitching and free motion straight stitching.

7 ▪ Use a soft brown or taupe thread to outline the facial features and beard. If desired, add some white stitching on the beard for contrast and texture. Don't forget to highlight the eyes; that's what brings Santa to life.

DESIGN: LORI KERR
SIZE: 12" x 17½" (30.5 x 44.5 CM)

FIGURE 1

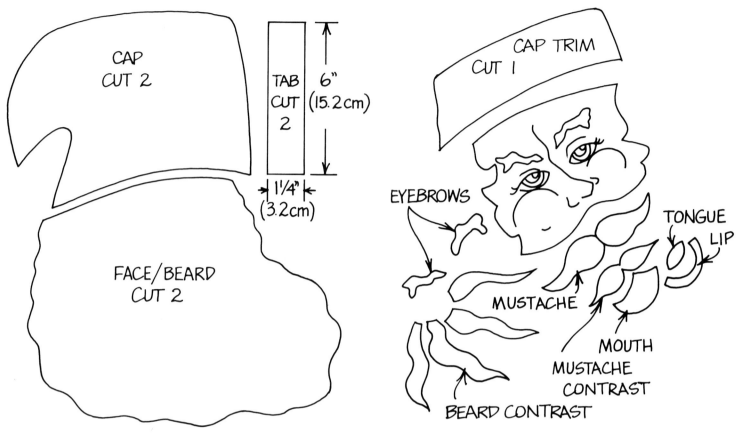

CAP
CUT 2

TAB
CUT
2

6"
(15.2 cm)

1¼"
(3.2 cm)

FACE/BEARD
CUT 2

CAP TRIM
CUT 1

EYEBROWS

TONGUE
LIP

MUSTACHE

MOUTH
MUSTACHE
CONTRAST

BEARD CONTRAST

8 ▪ After completing the creative stitching, construct the stocking by putting the right sides together and sewing ¼" (6-mm) seams. Sew the sides and bottom, but leave the top open. Make sure to clip all the curves. Repeat with the lining. With the right sides together, sew the long edges of the tab; then turn it right side out.

9 ▪ Press both pieces and place the lining inside the outer stocking. Position the tab where desired and turn in the upper edges ⅜" (1 cm). Edge-stitch together.

10 ▪ To make the star at the end of the hat, trace the design onto the right side of the desired fabric. Use fusible web to bond this to another piece of the fabric, adding a piece of tear-away interfacing between the two. Outline the star in satin stitching; then cut the star very close to the stitching. Sew it in place on the hat.

11 ▪ Lightly shade Santa's cheeks with pink colored pencil.

FIGURE 2

CHRISTMAS TREE SKIRT

In this delightful tree skirt, Kim Tibbals fashioned her Santa in profile with wave upon wave of beard. He strikes a man-in-the-moon pose amidst a star-filled night sky.

DESIGN: KIM TIBBALS
SIZE: 60" (1.5 M) DIAMETER

MATERIALS & TOOLS

- 3⅓ yds. (3 m) royal blue felt
- yardstick or long straightedge
- straight pins
- pinking shears
- gold metallic thread
- sewing machine
- 1 yd. (91.4 cm) white felt
- ½ yd. (45.7 cm) red felt
- 12" (30.5-cm) square pale pink felt
- 12" square rosy pink felt
- scrap of pale blue felt
- temporary fabric marker
- 18 wooden stars 2¼" (5.7 cm) in diameter
- 14 wooden stars 1" (2.5 cm) in diameter
- electric drill with ¹⁄₁₆" (2-mm) bit
- gold metallic craft paint
- paintbrush
- large-eyed sharp needle
- 4½ yds. (4.1 m) gold metallic cord
- 18" (45.7 cm) gold metallic wired ribbon
- 2" to 3" (5.1- to 7.6-cm) white pompon
- 2 gold jingle bells
- 18" gold metallic braid (¾" / 1.9 cm or wider)
- fabric glue
- fray retardant liquid
- black chenille stem
- gold metallic fabric paint in squeeze bottle

INSTRUCTIONS

1 ▪ Fold the blue felt in half widthwise and cut it into two 60" (1.5-m) squares. Using pinking shears, cut each square into a 60" circle. (Fold the square in half and mark the center point on the fold. Placing one end of a yardstick at the center, pivot it to mark out the circle with straight pins.)

2 ▪ Make button loops from the scraps by cutting three strips 1¼" x 7" (3.2 x 17.8 cm) with pinking shears. Fold each in half lengthwise and stitch ¼" (6 mm) from the edge with metallic thread. Then fold each in half widthwise and stitch across the raw edges.

FIGURE 1

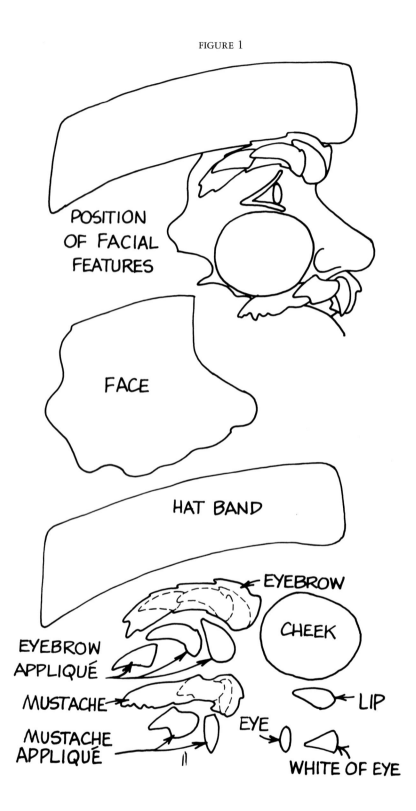

3 ▪ Enlarge the patterns in *figure 1* and cut the following pieces from the colors indicated: cheek and lip (rosy pink); hat (red); face (pale pink); eye (pale blue); hat band, white of eye, eyebrow and three appliqué pieces, mustache and two appliqué pieces, hair/beard and eight to ten irregularly shaped appliqué pieces (white). All are cut using pinking shears.

4 ▪ Starting with the beard and hat, position the pieces onto one of the blue circles as shown in the photo. Place the large pieces first; then add the smaller details and appliqué pieces, saving the eye pieces for later. Once you're satisfied, secure them with pins.

5 ▪ Stitch the pieces in place using metallic thread and a ¼" (6-mm) seam. Sew the underlying pieces first, working slowly to prevent slippage. The metallic thread is prone to breaking, so be patient with it. Stitch just two-thirds of the way up the right side of the hat, leaving the top open to fold down later, and do *not* stitch around the outer edge of the circle.

6 ▪ Pin the second blue circle to the back side of the appliquéd one, carefully aligning the outer edges. Turn the skirt right side up and mark the center point with a pin. Then draw a straight line from the center to the outer edge wherever you want the back opening. Cut through both thicknesses with pinking shears. Using a small plate as a guide, draw a 6" (15.2-cm) circle in the exact center of the tree skirt. Pin the open edges together. Place the button loops along the back opening, slipping the raw edges between the two felt layers, and pin.

7 ▪ Stitch the two circles together along all the open edges using metallic thread and a ½" (1.3-cm) seam. Break the stitching at the top end of the hat to allow it to fold down.

8 ▪ Make buttons from all the stars by drilling two holes ¼" (6 mm) apart in the center of each. Then paint them gold. Using a large-eyed needle and gold cord, sew them in a random arrangement, using three of the larger ones for buttons. Insert the needle down through a star, through the top layer of blue felt, and back up through the star. Tie a knot and knot the ends of the cord.

9 ▪ Using a double strand of metallic thread, tack the tip of the hat in place. Add a ribbon bow, two jingle bells, and the pompon at the tip of the hat. Glue the gold trim along the bottom of the hat with fabric glue and seal the ends with fray retardant.

10 ▪ Form the eye by bending and cutting the chenille stem into a V that slightly overextends the white of the eye. Position the white and blue eye pieces and the black V; then glue them in place.

11 ▪ Using a temporary marker as a guide, write a Christmas greeting along the outer edge of the skirt, beginning at the end of the beard. Then trace the lettering with gold fabric paint.

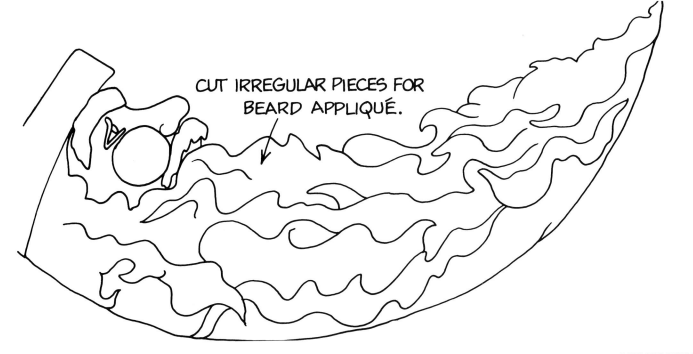

CUT IRREGULAR PIECES FOR BEARD APPLIQUÉ.

WINDSOCK SANTA

Marj Beaty designed this playful Santa with long spidery legs to keep him dancing even in the lightest of breezes. With his charming demeanor and bulging bag of gifts, he's certain to waltz his way into the hearts of all your holiday guests.

MATERIALS & TOOLS

- 3 strips of plastic boning, each 21" (53.3 cm) long
- ⅝ yd. (57.2 cm) red banner fabric
- ⅛ yd. (11.4 cm) artificial fur
- ⅛ yd. (11.4 cm) black vinyl fabric
- ⅛ yd. (11.4 cm) curtain lace
- pinking shears
- scraps of muslin
- polyester fiberfill
- decorative thread: red, black, white, and off-white
- lamb's wool
- fabric paint pens
- soft red pencil
- white satin ribbon 20" (50.8 cm) long
- 1½ yds. (1.4 m) gold cord
- net or string bag or small onion bag
- Christmas gift wrap and ribbon
- 20-gauge copper wire

DESIGN: MARJORIE INGALLS BEATY
SIZE: 6½" x 27½" (16.5 x 69.9 CM)

INSTRUCTIONS

1 ▪ Bend each strip of plastic boning into a circle and overlap the ends by about ½" (1.3 cm). After tacking the ends, assemble all three circles into a ball and secure them at top and bottom with needle and thread. This forms the framework for Santa's body.

2 ▪ Measure and cut five sections of banner fabric to fit over the framework (*fig. 1*). The measurements shown include a ¼" (6-mm) seam allowance on each side. With the right sides together, sew the sections together, leaving one seam open for turning. Clip the curves, turn, and press. Then insert the frame into the fabric shell. Hand-stitch the final seam closed.

3 ▪ Using pinking shears, cut two 2"-diameter (5.1-cm) circles of banner fabric. Stitch one on top and bottom of the ball to finish it.

4 ▪ Cut a 6" (15.2-cm) circle of muslin for the head. Gather it around the edge and fill it with enough fiberfill to make a head about 2½" (6.4 cm) in diameter. Tie the neckline with heavy thread so that there is a 1" to 2" (2.5- to 5.1-cm) bib at the bottom.

5 ▪ Cut a ¾"-diameter (1.9-cm) circle of muslin and gather it around the edge. Lightly stuff it with fiberfill to make a nose. Then stitch the nose to the face. Draw the other facial features with fabric paint pens and add touches of "rouge" with the soft red pencil.

6 ▪ Attach the head to the body by stitching the muslin bib to the banner fabric. To add the hair, beard, and mustache, sew or hot-glue pieces of curly wool to the head and face (*fig. 2*).

7 ▪ With pinking shears, cut a 6" (15.2-cm) circle from red banner fabric. Make a single cut from the edge of the circle to the center, fit the piece over the muslin bib, and tack it together at the back. Then cut the circle into 1"-wide (2.5-cm) streamers, cutting to within 1" (2.5 cm) of the neckline.

8 ▪ Cut a 4" (10.2-cm) circle from curtain lace using pinking shears. After making a cut into the center, place it around the neckline and tack it at the back.

9 ▪ To make the legs, use pinking shears to cut a 16" x 20" (40.6 x 50.8 cm) rectangle of banner fabric. Then cut a series of 1"-wide (2.5-cm) streamers to within 1½" (3.8 cm) of one 20" (50.8-cm) edge. Wrap the uncut edge around Santa's waist and tack it in place. Attach a 2"-wide (5.1-cm) strip of fur around the waist to make a belt.

10 ▪ Cut four boots from the black vinyl. With wrong sides together, hand-stitch the outer edges of each pair, leaving the top open.

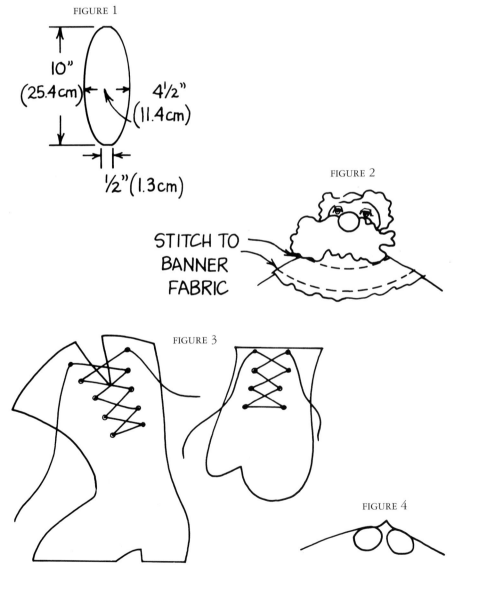

FIGURE 1

10" (25.4cm)

4½" (11.4cm)

½" (1.3cm)

FIGURE 2

STITCH TO BANNER FABRIC

FIGURE 3

FIGURE 4

11 ▪ To form the legs, divide the streamers into two equal clusters. Pin them together at each pant leg cuff. Then tuck each batch into a boot and pin. Using doubled red decorative thread, sew laces up the front of the boots to hold the streamers in place (*fig. 3*).

12 ▪ Cut two gloves from black vinyl and one long strip 1" x 18" (2.5 x 45.7 cm) from red banner fabric. Attach a glove to each end of the strip with red thread "laces." Attach the center of the red strip under the lace bib and tack the arms at the shoulders.

13 ▪ For Santa's hat, cut a 6" (15.2-cm) square of banner fabric. Cut a 1½" x 6" (3.8- x 15.2-cm) strip of fur. With right sides together, stitch the fur to one edge of the square. After turning out the fur, fold the square in half with the wrong sides together. The fur should be at the bottom edge. Machine-stitch diagonally from the fold to the outside edge of the fur. Trim to leave a ¼" (6-mm) seam and turn. Attach a small piece of fur at the peak of the hat.

14 ▪ Santa's gifts can be small jewelry boxes or polystyrene squares wrapped with Christmas paper. Add a few fabric stars or other lightweight items to fill the onion bag. Tie the bag with gold cord and tack the cord to Santa's glove at one shoulder. Tack the other glove to Santa's belt.

15 ▪ Complete Santa's adornment with a white satin or French ribbon bow tied around the neck. Fashion glasses from copper wire, wrapping it around a dowel or pencil to obtain two equal circles (*fig. 4*). Tuck the ends under the hat and tack them in place. Tie a piece of gold cord 18" (45.7 cm) or longer to the hat so that you can hang your Santa windsock where he will greet your holiday guests.

CATCHING A FEW WINKS

Designed by Dana Irwin and hooked by Laura Dover, this delightful rug would be equally attractive displayed on a wall or at the hearth. Joining Santa in slumber is Laura's chocolate Labrador, Emma; when you make your own rug, feel free to substitute your family pet.

MATERIALS & TOOLS

- primitive (loose weave) burlap, 38" x 22" (96.5 x 55.9 cm)
- ¾ yd. (68.6 cm) blue wool
- ½ yd. (45.7 cm) green wool
- 1 yd. (91.4 cm) gray wool
- ⅛ yd. (11.4 cm) each of red, dark brown, black, ivory, and brown-and-white herringbone or tweed wool
- scraps of light brown, yellow, and pink wool
- tracing paper and tracing wheel or piece of soft charcoal
- rotary cutter and/or sewing scissors
- primitive hook
- basic lap frame
- 1 package twill binding tape
- needle and thread

INSTRUCTIONS

1 ▪ Enlarge the design shown in *figure 1* by 510% or to the size desired.

2 ▪ Transfer the design to your burlap. One method is to use pattern tracing paper and a tracing wheel. Another is to place the enlargement face down against a sunny window and, on the reverse side, trace the pattern with a piece of soft charcoal or an iron-on transfer pen. Place the enlargement tracing

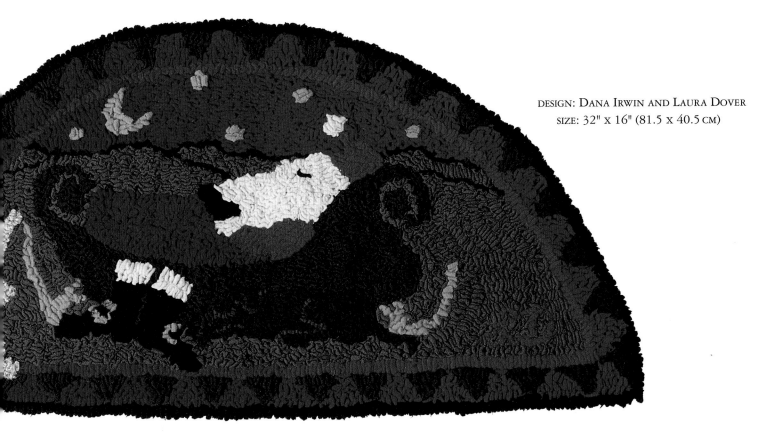

DESIGN: DANA IRWIN AND LAURA DOVER
SIZE: 32" x 16" (81.5 x 40.5 CM)

side down on the burlap and transfer the design to the burlap. If you use a transfer pen, a hot iron will be required to transfer the image. Be sure to leave a 2" to 3" (5.1- to 7.6-cm) border of plain burlap around the design.

3 ▪ Use a sharp cutter or sewing scissors to cut your fabric into strips. For this rug, the wool was cut into ¼" (6-mm) strips for most of the design. Strips ⅛" (3 mm) wide were used for detail areas such as Santa's face and the shading of the dog.

4 ▪ Mount your canvas in the lap frame and begin hooking the rug. Start in the center with Santa in his sleigh. Hook the border next, then the rest of the design. Fill in the background last.

5 ▪ To finish the rug, trim the burlap border to ¾" (1.9 cm) and fold twill binding tape over the edge all around, stitching it in place by hand or machine. Place a damp towel over the rug and iron it on both sides. Let it dry for at least 24 hours; then fold the edges over so that none of the burlap is visible. Carefully sew the finished edges to the back of the rug.

FIGURE 1

SANTA'S SAMPLER

Peggy Hayes designed this sampler to welcome guests of all nationalities to your home for the holidays. Use the last line to personalize your sampler with your own name (or that of the person for whom you're making it) or with your own favorite holiday greeting.

MATERIALS & TOOLS

- 14-count Aida cloth in mushroom color 14½" x 16½" (36.8 x 41.9 cm)
- tapestry needle
- **DMC COLORS (1 SKEIN OF EACH)**
  white
  ecru
  darkest cranberry #815
  light creamy peach #754
  country blue denim #930
  medium country blue #932
  dark pistachio #367
  light honey #676
  dark country blue #931
  dark spruce #890
  medium pistachio #320
  dark honey #680
  dark golden brown #434
  darkest silver #317
  medium pecan #840
  medium silver #318
  gold metallic embroidery thread

INSTRUCTIONS

1 ▪ Mark the horizontal and vertical center of the canvas with basting thread.

2 ▪ Using two strands of floss in your needle, cross-stitch the design according to the chart. Back-stitch (outline-stitch) the lettering in two strands of darkest silver, snowflakes in two strands of medium country blue, small border in two strands of dark golden brown, and center of the large border in one strand of gold metallic thread.

3 ▪ Using two strands of the same color floss, back-stitch around these completed designs: hat; eyes; large green, gold, and blue presents; small presents in sampler; bells in sampler; and small border. Use two strands of medium pecan to back-stitch around the fur on the hat and gloves. Back-stitch around the hair, beard, mustache, eyebrows, and face with two strands of medium silver.

4. For the ribbons on all of the presents, back-stitch in extra-long stitches with gold metallic thread. Tie a bow with gold metallic thread on the large blue present.

5. Make two French knots over the *e* in Noël and a single French knot under each bell. Sew a glass seed bead at the top of each Christmas tree.

6. Stretch and frame the finished needlework as desired.

KEY TO CHART

＼	= Dark Spruce
∩	= Darkest Cranberry
■	= Country Blue Denim
●	= Light Honey
∩	= Dark Golden Brown
⊔	= Light Creamy Peach
⊐	= Dark Country Blue
—	= Dark Honey
·	= White
⊏	= Medium Pistachio
V	= Ecru
I	= Medium Country Blue
／	= Dark Pistachio

DESIGN: MARGARET (PEGGY) HAYES
SIZE: 6⅜" x 8⅜" (16.2 x 21.9 CM), DESIGN AREA

Merry Christmas

Feliz Navidad

Joyeux Noel

Frohe Weihnachten

Your Name Here

TRADITIONAL FIGURES

HARLEQUIN SANTA

Because he's the object of everyone's affection, designers Nan and Bill Parker decided that Santa deserved to be placed on a pedestal. They've shown him here in a bright, theatrical costume, which demonstrates his flair for making a dramatic entrance every Christmas.

DESIGN: NAN AND BILL PARKER
SIZE: 24" (61 CM) TALL

MATERIALS & TOOLS

- 4" (10.2-cm) wooden egg
- acrylic paints
- small and medium paintbrushes
- 1 package white polymer clay
- craft glue
- matte acrylic spray sealer
- wood baluster or other pillar 1½" x 19" (3.8 x 48.3 cm)
- wood base 6" x 4" (15.2 x 10.2 cm)
- crackle medium
- scrap of black fabric
- 18-gauge wire
- polyester fiberfill
- ½ yd. (45.7 cm) taffeta
- electric drill with ⅛" (3-mm) bit
- unbleached lamb's wool
- gold trim
- scrap of velvet
- sprigs of preserved cedar and dried flowers
- 27" (68.6 cm) upholstery cord with tassels

INSTRUCTIONS

1 ■ Begin the head by applying two coats of flesh-colored paint to the wooden egg, allowing the paint to dry between coats. Then paint the eyes, mouth, and cheeks.

2 ■ Construct a simple nose using polymer clay. Bake it according to the manufacturer's guidelines and glue the cooled piece to the face. Then paint it to match the rest of the face. When you're satisfied with the painting, spray the entire face with matte acrylic sealer.

3 ■ Apply a base coat of metallic or acrylic gold paint to the wood pillar. After it has dried thoroughly, brush on an even coat of crackle medium. Follow the manufacturer's instructions for drying time; then apply the red paint. This will crackle within seconds, but let it dry well before spraying the pillar with acrylic sealer.

4 ■ Paint the wood base with at least two coats of black acrylic paint.

5 ■ Using wood glue, attach the head to the pillar and the pillar to the base.

6 ■ From the black fabric, cut four arm pieces according to the pattern in *figure 1*. Be sure to add seam allowances to all pattern pieces. Sew the side seams with right sides together. Trim the seams, clip the curves, turn, and press. Cut two pieces of wire, each 23" (58.4 cm) long, and bend them in half. Insert the rounded end of each wire into an arm. Then stuff the arms with fiberfill. Turn under the raw edge on each arm and gather it with a loose basting stitch.

7 ■ Cut the sleeves from taffeta and stitch the seams. Turn under the edges at both ends and sew them with a gathering stitch. After inserting some fiberfill into the top part of each sleeve, pull the thread to gather the fabric at both ends, leaving an opening large enough to accommodate Santa's arm.

8 ■ To attach the arms to the body, drill a hole on each side of the pillar 2" (5.1 cm) down from the head. Insert the arm wires and glue the ends into the holes. Once the glue is dry, carefully slip the sleeves onto the arms. Position the fabric at the shoulders as desired, and hot-glue the sleeves to the pillar.

9 ■ Create the beard, mustache, and hair by gluing pieces of lamb's wool to the face and head.

10 ■ Sew two hat pieces together at the side seams. After turning the hat right side out, fold under the bottom edge and stitch gold trim around the hem. If desired, stuff some fiberfill into the hat and insert a piece of wire to stiffen it further. The wire will allow you to arrange the hat in any position you wish. Then glue the hat onto the head.

11 ▪ For Santa's bag, cut two rectangles of velvet, each 4" x 10" (10.2 x 25.4 cm). With the right sides together, stitch the seam all around except on one 4" edge. Press under the remaining edge and tack it in place. After turning the bag right side out, fill it lightly with fiberfill and glue in some pieces of preserved cedar and dried flowers. Loop the upholstery cord over Santa's arm and tie it in a bow around the bag. Glue additional dried materials to the front of the bag to complete its decoration.

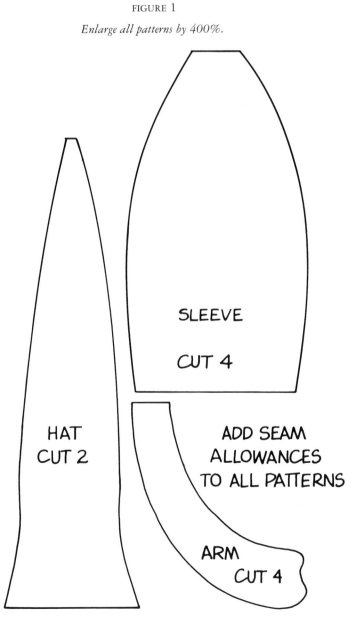

FIGURE 1

Enlarge all patterns by 400%.

SLEEVE

CUT 4

HAT
CUT 2

ADD SEAM
ALLOWANCES
TO ALL PATTERNS

ARM
CUT 4

ENGLISH PEDDLER SANTA

Virginia Killmore created this Old World figure to fulfill every child's dream of a Santa laden with gifts and treats for the whole family. He is made almost entirely of fabric—the exception is his simple wooden armature—with a painted muslin face and a robe cut from the remnant of an old quilt.

DESIGN: VIRGINIA KILLMORE
SIZE: 16" (40.6 CM) TALL

MATERIALS & TOOLS

- wooden base 5" x 5" (12.7 x 12.7 cm)
- piece of wood 1" x 2¼" x 10¼" (2.5 x 5.7 x 26 cm)
- 1½" (3.8-cm) wood screws
- wood stain
- ⅓ yd. (30.5 cm) quilt remnant
- ⅓ yd. (30.5 cm) lining
- ¼ yd. (22.9 cm) lightweight fabric
- ⅛ yd. (11.4 cm) face-colored muslin
- ⅓ yd. (30.5 cm) wool fabric
- fabric paint pens
- polyester fiberfill
- 2 pieces 16-gauge wire 18" (45.7 cm) long
- staple gun
- glue gun
- 21" (53.3 cm) gold cord
- 1 gold tassel
- lamb's wool or roving
- 28" (71.1-cm) strand of tiny gold beads
- 3" (7.6-cm) twig or vine wreath
- dried greenery
- assorted miniature toys

INSTRUCTIONS

1 • Assemble the armature by standing the 10¼" (26-cm) piece of wood in the center of the base and securing the two together with wood screws. Apply a light coating of stain and allow it to dry.

2 • To make the robe, cut a rectangle 12" x 16" (30.5 x 40.6 cm) from the quilt remnant. Remove the quilt batting and any extra threads; then use the pattern in *figure 1* to cut slots for the sleeves. Cut an identical piece from the lining fabric. Fold the front section to the back, placing right sides together, and sew the shoulder seams on both the coat and the lining. With right sides together, sew the lining to the coat, starting at the upper right front, continuing around the hemline, and back up to the left front. Turn the robe right side out and press. Then tack the seams together at the neckline.

3 • For the sleeves, cut two pieces each 8" x 7" (20.3 x 17.8 cm) from the quilt remnant and the lining. With right sides together, sew the lining to the sleeve at the cuff. Open the two pieces; then sew the side seam together across the sleeve and lining, making a long tube. Use a ⅜" (1-cm) seam for all sewing. Turn the tube right side out and fold the lining into the sleeve.

4 • Placing the right sides together, sew the sleeves to the coat at the openings, easing the sleeves as necessary. Turn and press.

5 • For the hood, cut one piece of quilt and one of lining according to the pattern. With right sides together, sew the lining to the quilt along the front (the two 5"/12.7-cm edges). Clip the curves; then turn and press. With the lining facing out, fold the hood in half and sew the back seam through all four layers. Turn the hood right side out, fold the front edge back to form a cuff, and press.

6 • Cut four mitten pieces according to the pattern. With right sides together, sew two together to make each hand. Turn the mittens right side out and press.

7 • Cut the lightweight fabric into a rectangle 12" x 7½" (30.5 x 19 cm) for the undergarment. Hem all four sides.

8 • To make the unhemmed shawl that drapes over Santa's arms, cut a piece of wool as indicated in the pattern. Roll it lengthwise, making it about 1½" to 2" (3.8 to 5.1 cm) wide, and set it aside.

9 • Sew two pieces together for the head, leaving the bottom open. Turn the head right side out and stuff it with fiberfill. Then draw in the facial features with paint pens.

10 • Begin the assembly by gluing and stapling the head to the top of the armature. Bend both pieces of wire in half for the arms. Staple the ends of each arm to one side of the base at a point 8¼" (21 cm) up from the bottom. Then bend the wires down to create the arms. Wrap fiberfill around the arms and upper chest area and hot-glue it in place. Slip the mittens gently over the wires to keep the fiberfill in place. Secure with glue.

11 • To dress your Santa, wrap the undergarment around the body just under the arms, and glue it together at the back. Its bottom edge should barely touch the base. Place the robe on the figure, gluing it closed under the chin and along the front of the chest. Attach the tassels to the gold cord to make a belt. Tie it around the waistline and tack it in place with glue.

12 • Glue pieces of wool around the head area to create hair. To attach the hood, match the center back seam with the center back of the robe. Fold the raw edges up and tack the hood in place. Continue gluing around one side of the head, making sure the raw edges are facing up. Tack the front cuff just under the chin area; then repeat on the other side. Bring the hood up and tack it to the top of the head so that it lies naturally. Glue pieces of wool onto the face for a beard and mustache.

13 • Carefully adjust the arms and drape the shawl across them in a graceful curve. Then drape the strand of gold beads on top of the shawl. Tack both in place with glue. Glue the wreath in one hand. Add bunches of greenery to fill the shawl and glue them in place, together with assorted small toys and ornaments.

FIGURE 1

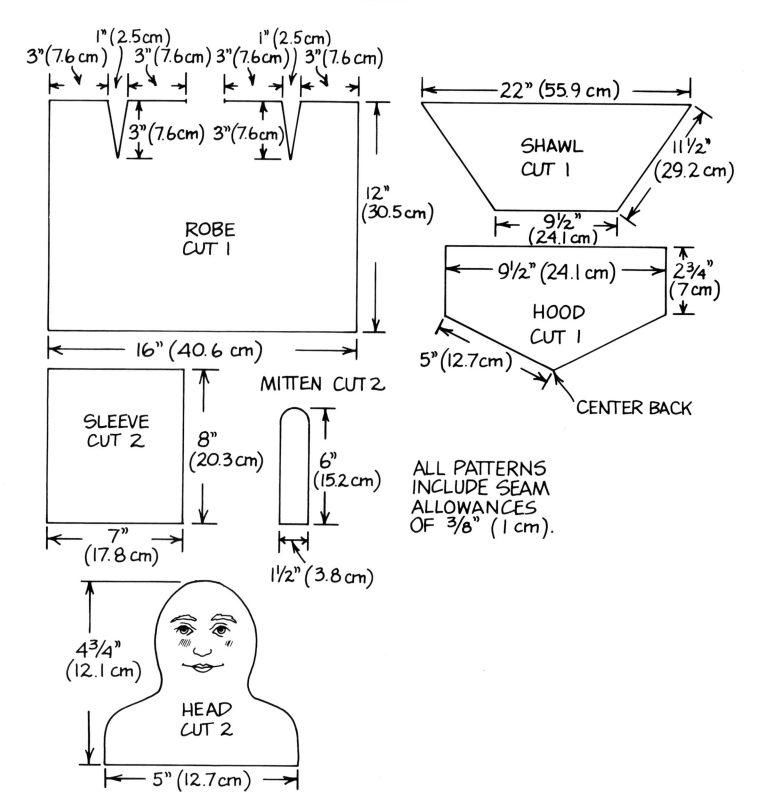

PINECONE FATHER CHRISTMAS

With his body made of cones, leather vest, and miniature feather tree, this figure was very popular during the Victorian period. Pat Scheible has added a contemporary touch by substituting polymer clay for the original papier-mâché head, hands, and boots.

MATERIALS & TOOLS

- 5 fir cones
- 20-gauge wire
- 2 packages of white or gray polymer clay
- acrylic paints
- artist's brush
- glue gun and hot glue
- polyester batting
- scraps of wool, leather, and sheepskin
- a few locks of white kid mohair
- small artificial tree
- onion bag
- miniature toys and other trinkets

DESIGN: PAT SCHEIBLE
SIZE: 12" (30.5 CM) TALL

INSTRUCTIONS

1 ▪ Wire the cones together to form the body with arms and legs (*fig. 1*).

2 ▪ Condition the polymer clay by manipulating it in your hands for several minutes until it is easily pliable. Matching the scale of your cones, form a head with neck and shoulders; then make two hands and two boots. The neck and shoulders won't show when the piece is finished, but they will make it easier to attach the head to the cone body. Don't worry if the face and hands you model look less than perfect; that only adds to their character.

3 ▪ Bake the polymer clay pieces according to the manufacturer's instructions. Once they've cooled, paint each piece with acrylic paints. Then attach them to the body with hot glue. .

4 ▪ Pad the torso with a few strips of polyester batting, securing the ends with hot glue.

5 ▪ Cut a wool tunic and leather vest according to the patterns in *figure 2* and stitch them in place on the padded torso.

6 ▪ Cut a simple hat from the wool, stitch it at the seam, and glue it onto the head. Using a glue gun, attach a narrow strip of sheepskin around the bottom edge.

7 ▪ Glue locks of mohair onto the face for the beard, hair, and eyebrows.

8 ▪ Add the tools of Santa's trade by gluing the small tree in one hand and attaching the onion bag full of trinkets on the opposite shoulder.

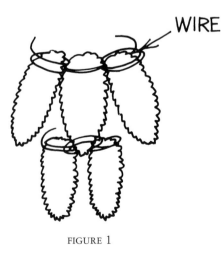

FIGURE 1

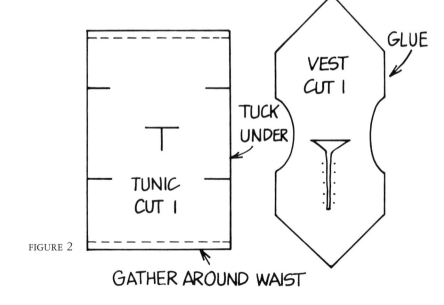

FIGURE 2

CHRISTMAS TREE SANTA

Dana Irwin based this figure on an antique ornament that has been in her family for generations. Using a ribbon sash around his waist, the Santa is tied into the Christmas tree and nestled among the branches.

MATERIALS & TOOLS

- small-gauge chicken wire
- needle-nose pliers
- wire cutter
- small piece quilted fabric
- needle and thread
- instant papier-mâché
- plastic wrap
- rolling pin
- modeling tool
- ⅓ yd. (30.5 cm) red felt
- polyester beard material, fur, or lamb's wool
- acrylic paints
- artist's brush
- herb sprig
- 1⅔ yds. (1.5 m) narrow fabric ribbon
- clear glitter
- glue gun

INSTRUCTIONS

1 ▪ Crush the chicken wire into the rough shape of a head, body, and arms (*fig. 1*). Use the wire cutter as needed to separate portions of the wire to form the arms and turn one arm upward with the pliers.

2 ▪ To give Santa a rounded figure, wrap a piece of quilted fabric around the body portion of the armature and tack it in place with needle and thread.

3 ▪ Prepare the instant papier-mâché according to the package instructions. Place a ball of pulp between two pieces of plastic wrap and flatten it into a sheet about ¼" (6 mm) thick using the rolling pin. Wrap portions of the sheet over the head and hands, smoothing them with dampened fingers. Allow this layer to dry overnight.

DESIGN: DANA IRWIN
SIZE: 11½" (29.2 CM) TALL

4 ▪ Using small dabs of papier-mâché, form the facial features and shape the hands. Dampen your fingers or modeling tool before using it to prevent the pulp from sticking. Don't worry if the face and hands aren't perfectly smooth; the rough texture adds to the aged appearance.

5 ▪ While the papier-mâché is drying, cut the pattern pieces for the hooded robe as indicated in *figure 2*. Be sure to add seam allowances and hems where necessary. Sew the side and shoulder seams of the robe and the front and back seams of the hood, leaving the bottom front open. Then sew the hood to the neck, easing any fullness at the neck.

6 ▪ When the papier-mâché is completely dry, paint the face and hands with acrylic paints. The eyes are the most distinct feature and most important. *Figure 3* shows one method for painting the eyes.

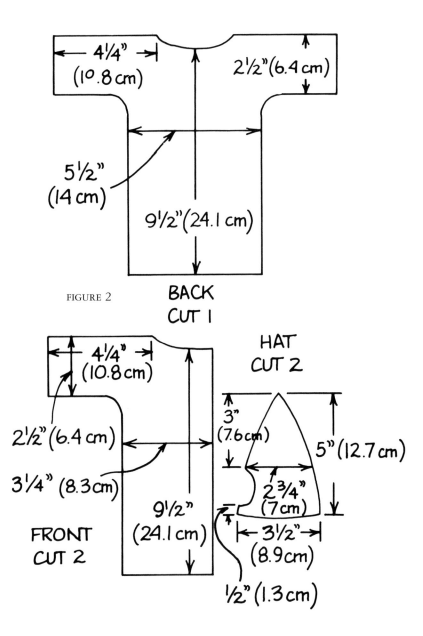

FIGURE 2

7 ▪ In the original antique version, Santa's beard is made of fur, and the Santa pictured here has a beard made of polyester fibers. Using either of these or lamb's wool, hot-glue a beard to Santa's face.

8 ▪ Glue an herb sprig in one hand and attach a ribbon around Santa's waist, leaving the long ends free to tie around the Christmas tree. Then give him a sprinkling of snow on the shoulders and head by gluing clear glitter to his robe.

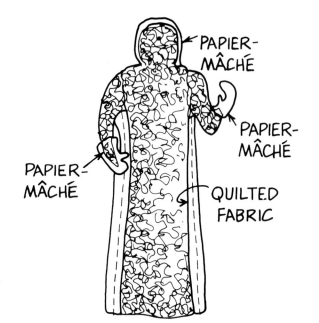

FIGURE 1

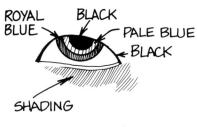

FIGURE 3

ONDROUS SAINT

This saintly figure has a rapturous expression as he contemplates the night sky and his long journey ahead. Designer Christi Hensley achieves this glow by dipping the painted papier-mâché face into a bath of melted wax.

DESIGN: CHRISTI HENSLEY
SIZE: 23" (58.4 CM) HIGH

MATERIALS & TOOLS

- aluminum foil
- instant papier-mâché
- sandpaper
- gesso sealer
- acrylic paints
- artist's brushes
- 2 lbs. (908 g) candle wax
- coffee can
- lamb's wool
- poster board
- glue gun
- ½ yd. (45.7 cm) fabric for undergarment
- 1½ yd. (1.4 m) upholstery fabric
- ½ yd. (45.7 cm) trim fabric
- sewing machine and thread (optional)
- polyester fiberfill
- strong rubber band
- scrap of black fabric
- ½ yd. (45.7 cm) burlap
- 23" (58.4 cm) stick
- pinecones and berries
- decorative cord with tassel

INSTRUCTIONS

1 ▪ Form a 3" (7.6-cm) ball of aluminum foil, leaving a neck stem about ½" (1.3 cm) wide and 1½" (3.8 cm) long (*fig. 1*).

2 ▪ Mix the instant papier-mâché according to the manufacturer's directions and apply a coating about ¼" (6 mm) thick over the aluminum base. After the initial layer has dried, model the nose, cheeks, and mouth. Creating the features may take a few layers; allow the papier-mâché to dry between applications.

3 ▪ To prepare the head for painting, smooth it with sandpaper and apply two coats of gesso. Use a skin tone as a base coat over the entire head. After this has dried, paint on the features, using the photograph as a guide.

4 ▪ Place the wax in a coffee can and heat it in a pan of hot water until it reaches a temperature of about 190°F (90°C). Holding the head by the neck, dip it into the wax as far as possible. Remove the head in one continuous movement, tilting the features up so that any excess wax drips to the back. Let the wax harden and dip again.

5 ▪ Glue won't stick to wax, so scrape the beard, hair, and eyebrow areas. Attach the wool at these points with hot glue.

6 ▪ Trim the poster board to 28" x 18" (71.1 x 45.7 cm) and form it into a cone with a 1" (2.5-cm) opening at the top and a 9" (22.9-cm) opening at the bottom. After securing it with hot glue, trim the cone so that it will stand (*fig. 2*).

7 ▪ To cover the body of the figure, cut a piece of fabric 9" x 21" (22.9 x 53.3 cm) for the undergarment. Glue this lengthwise to the front of the cone, tucking under the edges at the top and bottom and gluing them to the inside of the cone. Cut a piece of coat fabric 21" x 40" (53.3 x 101.6 cm) and two pieces of trim fabric 6" x 21" (15.2 x 53.3 cm). Sew or glue the trim to the shorter edges of the coat. Then fold each piece of trim in half lengthwise and hem or glue the raw edge to the inside of the coat.

8 ▪ Cut one 7" x 21" (17.8- x 53.3-cm) piece of coat fabric for the arms. Cut two pieces of trim fabric 5" x 7" (12.7 x 17.8 cm) and sew or glue these to the short edges. Then fold the trim and hem or glue it to the wrong side of the fabric. With the right sides together, fold the sleeve in half lengthwise and make a seam. Turn the right side out and lightly stuff the tube with polyester. Now mark the center; each half becomes an arm.

9 ▪ For the hood, cut a 10" (25.4-cm) right triangle of coat fabric and a strip of trim 6" x 15" (15.2 x 38.1 cm). Attach the trim to the longer edge of the triangle, turning and hemming it as before. With right sides together, fold the triangle so that the equal sides meet. Sew down 5" (12.7 cm) from the right angle corner; then turn the piece right side out.

10 ▪ Attach the coat to the body by gathering it around the cone so that the front edges are slightly open to reveal the undergarment. Secure the gathers at the top of the cone with a strong rubber band, leaving about 1" of fabric above the top of the cone. After applying glue to the inside top edge of the cone, push the excess fabric into the opening.

11 ▪ To assemble the figure, attach the center of the arm piece to the center back of the coat at arm level. Glue the head into the top of the cone and place the hood. Turn and glue the raw edges at the front of the hood so that they are disguised by the beard. Make two mittens from the black fabric, add stuffing, and attach them to the arms. Using the burlap, cut a circle of fabric for the sack. Fill it with polyester and gather the edges with a decorative ribbon. Glue the sack onto the figure's back, covering the attachment of the arms, and glue one hand to the top of the bag. Glue the other hand to a stick decorated with pinecones, berries, and such. Finally, place a decorative cord with tassel around the saint's neck.

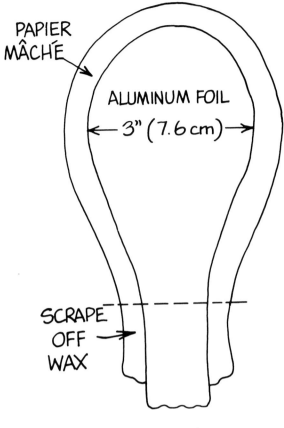

PAPIER
MÂCHÉ

ALUMINUM FOIL
3" (7.6 cm)

SCRAPE
OFF
WAX

FIGURE 1

FIGURE 2

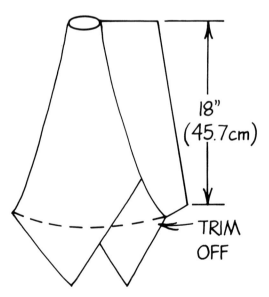

18"
(45.7cm)

TRIM
OFF

ROLY-POLY SANTA

Here is a Santa that fulfills all of our childhood expectations—he's got a twinkle in his eye, a pudgy tummy, and a hearty smile. Created by Mary Kay West, he's made almost entirely from stiffened fabric.

MATERIALS & TOOLS

- 3" (7.6-cm) dia. polystyrene ball
- 4" (10.2-cm) dia. polystyrene ball
- scrap of white knit fabric
- polystyrene glue
- ½ yd. (45.7 cm) red polar fleece or felt
- scraps of black cotton fabric
- scraps of white fabric
- sewing machine
- red and black thread
- polyester batting
- glue gun
- fabric stiffener
- latex gloves (recommended)
- medium paintbrush
- white embroidery floss
- small white tassel
- white fabric paint
- puff paints
- 2 blue seed beads
- 2-4 small buttons

DESIGN: MARY KAY WEST
SIZE: 12" (30.5 CM) TALL

INSTRUCTIONS

1 ▪ Cover the smaller foam ball with a piece of white knit fabric. (This provides a ready surface to use for attaching Santa's hair and beard later.) Then, using polystyrene glue, attach the smaller foam ball to the larger one.

2 ▪ Enlarge the patterns in *figure 1* and cut Santa's coat, pants, shoes, gloves, and hat. Sew the garments together, using a ⅜" (1-cm) seam. (All of the patterns shown include ⅜" seam allowances.)

3 ▪ "Dress" the polystyrene balls and stuff the arms, legs, shoes, gloves, and hat with polyester batting until the figure is filled out sufficiently. Secure the gloves into the sleeves and the shoes into the pant legs with hot glue or by tacking them in place with a needle and thread.

4 ▪ Position the hands where you'd like them to remain. Then hot-glue or sew them in place.

5 ▪ Dab the fabric stiffener onto Santa's entire outfit with a relatively stiff paintbrush and work it into the fabric with your fingers. Fabric stiffener irritates the skin, so wear a pair of latex gloves to protect your hands. Allow the stiffener to dry for at least 24 hours.

6 ▪ Cut strips of white fabric about ⅛" to ¼" (3 to 6 mm) wide to use for Santa's beard and hair. To secure the strips in place, tack or hot-glue them onto the knit fabric on Santa's head. Then use your fingers to apply fabric stiffener to the strips and curl them into position.

7 ▪ To make fur trim for the jacket, pants, and hat, hot-glue short pieces of embroidery floss to the fabric. Add a tassel to the point of the hat. Then apply stiffener to all the trim. After it has dried, fill any gaps with white fabric paint.

8 ▪ To make the face, apply puff paints to the fabric-covered foam ball. Build up the features, applying the paint in layers until you have sufficient thickness to model the features with toothpicks or other small sculpting tools. Place the seed beads in the eyes, using the holes for pupils.

9 ▪ Using white fabric paint and puff paint, add eyebrows and a mustache to the face. Stroke additional paint from the face onto the beard to make a smooth transition.

10 ▪ Hot-glue small buttons to the front of Santa's jacket to complete his attire.

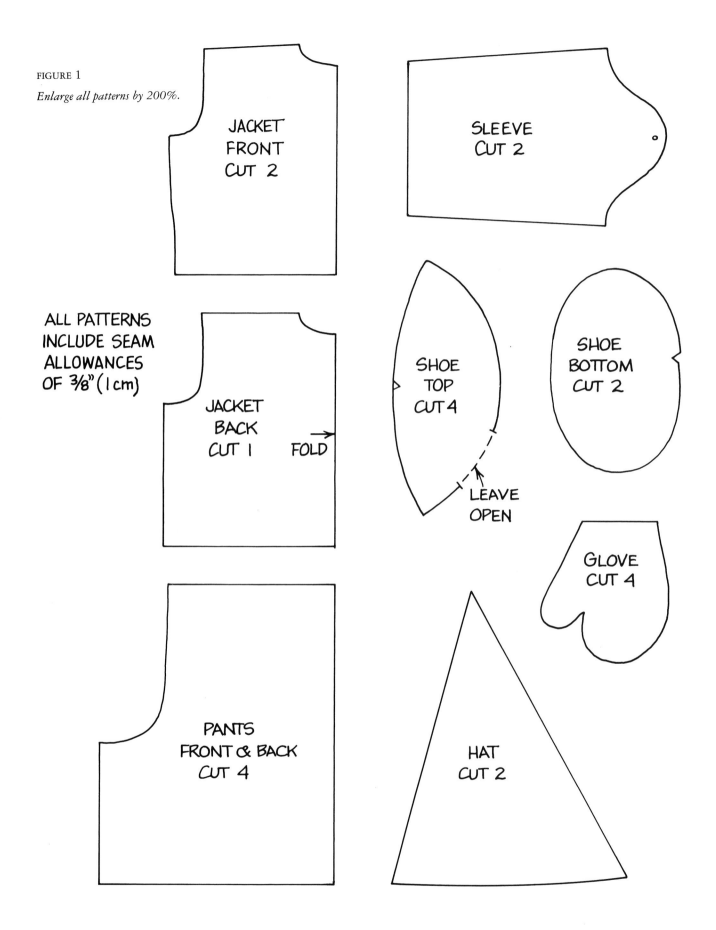

FIGURE 1

Enlarge all patterns by 200%.

JACKET
FRONT
CUT 2

SLEEVE
CUT 2

ALL PATTERNS
INCLUDE SEAM
ALLOWANCES
OF ⅜" (1 cm)

JACKET
BACK
CUT 1   → FOLD

SHOE
TOP
CUT 4

SHOE
BOTTOM
CUT 2

LEAVE
OPEN

GLOVE
CUT 4

PANTS
FRONT & BACK
CUT 4

HAT
CUT 2

WINTER'S EVE SANTA

Wearing a fur-trimmed brocade robe and carrying a garland of fruits and flowers, this Santa looks as though he's arrived just in time to join the holiday merriment. Don't let the rich fabrics deter you; Nan and Bill Parker created their figure using remnants they found in thrift stores.

DESIGN: NAN AND BILL PARKER
SIZE: 23" (58.4 CM) TALL

MATERIALS & TOOLS

- wooden pedestal 18" (45.7 cm) long
- 5" (12.7-cm) wooden ball
- 1 package white polymer clay
- acrylic paints
- small paintbrush
- craft glue
- drill with ¼" (6-mm) and ⅛" (3-mm) bits
- short piece of ¼" (6-mm) dowel
- carpenter's wood glue
- polyester batting
- glue gun
- scrap of black fabric
- 18-gauge wire
- polyester fiberfill
- ⅔ yd. (61 cm) damask or brocade
- ⅓ yd. (30.5 cm) gold lamé (optional)
- rabbit fur
- 27" (68.6 cm) upholstery cord with tassels
- 6 yds. (5.5 m) mohair yarn
- small piece of cardboard
- ⅓ yd. (30.5 cm) velvet
- gold trim
- spray of artificial leaves, fruits, and flowers

INSTRUCTIONS

1 ▪ Apply two coats of flesh-colored acrylic paint to the wooden pedestal and ball, allowing them to dry between coats.

2 ▪ Model a simple nose and mouth using the polymer clay and bake them according to the manufacturer's instructions. When they're cool, paint them with acrylic paints and glue them to the wooden ball. Paint the eyes directly on the head and shade the cheeks with pink paint.

3 ▪ Drill a ¼" (6-mm) hole in the base of the head and top of the body. Using wood glue, secure the short dowel into the head and body to hold them together. Then wrap the body with batting until Santa's figure is as full as you would like. Tack it in place with hot glue.

4 ▪ Using the patterns in *figure 1*, cut four pieces of black fabric for arms. Make sure to add seam allowances to all the pattern pieces before cutting. With right sides together, stitch the side seams. Trim the seams, clip the curves, turn, and press. Fold under the open ends and baste them with a loose gathering stitch.

5 ▪ Cut two pieces of wire, each 16" (40.6 cm) long. Bend the wires in half and insert one into each arm with the rounded end toward the hand. Then fill the arms with fiberfill and pull the gathered end close around the wire.

6 ▪ On each side of the pedestal, measure down 2" (5.1 cm) and drill a ⅛" (3-mm) hole. Insert the arm wires into the holes and glue the wires and ends of the arm fabric in place.

7 ▪ Cut two sleeves and two robe pieces from brocade fabric. If desired, cut pieces of gold lamé to make cuffs and a band at the bottom of the robe, as shown in the pattern. Be sure to add a seam allowance to the brocade and lamé pieces before cutting. Then attach the gold lamé to the brocade at the cuffs and hem.

8 ▪ Sew the robe pieces together at the shoulders; then sew the arm to the armhole, easing it to fit. On each side seam, sew from the end of the sleeve down to the bottom of the robe. Finish the neckline by turning under the raw edge and tacking it in place by hand. Hem the bottom edge of the robe.

9 ▪ After turning it right side out, complete the robe by gluing a strip of rabbit fur around the bottom hem and around each cuff. Then carefully place the robe on the figure, position the arms, and tie the upholstery cord around the waist.

10 ▪ Wrap the mohair yarn around a 5½"-long (14-cm) piece of cardboard 17 times. Using a piece of yarn, tie the loops together at the top; then cut them at the bottom. Slip the yarn off the cardboard and hot-glue it to Santa's face, arranging the pieces to give him a full beard. Glue a few short loops of yarn to the top of the head for hair and attach a small yarn mustache.

11 ▪ Cut two pieces of velvet for the hat. With right sides together, sew the side seams. Turn under the bottom edge and sew the gold trim around the hem on the right side of the fabric. If desired, insert a little fiberfill to give the hat some stiffness; then attach it to the head with hot glue.

12 ▪ Bend the artificial spray into a graceful curve and tack it to Santa's hands with hot glue.

FIGURE 1

Enlarge all pattern pieces by 400%.

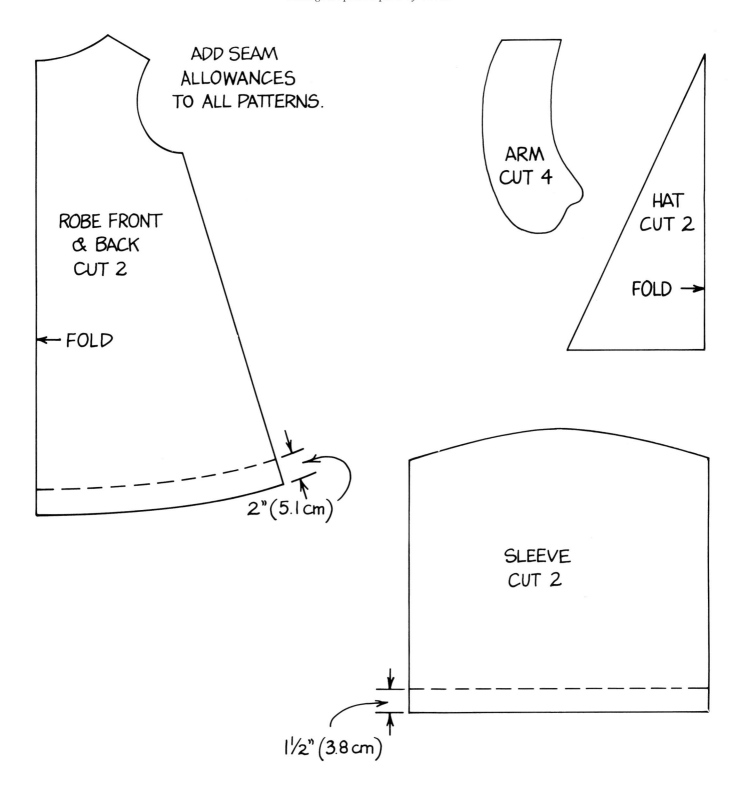

ADD SEAM
ALLOWANCES
TO ALL PATTERNS.

ROBE FRONT
& BACK
CUT 2

← FOLD

2" (5.1 cm)

ARM
CUT 4

HAT
CUT 2

FOLD →

SLEEVE
CUT 2

1½" (3.8 cm)

DESIGN: CAROL COSTENBADER   SIZE: 20" (50.8 CM) TALL

HEIRLOOM SANTA

Carol Costenbader began making her impressive Santa figures with the desire to use some of
the many fabrics and fur remnants that her mother had saved over the years. When you
make your own, you'll find that collecting the materials is half the fun.

MATERIALS & TOOLS

- wooden dowel ⅞" dia. x 12" long
  (2.2 x 30.5 cm)
- wooden dowel ¼" dia. x 2½" long
  (.6 x 6.4 cm)
- wooden base of your choice
- electric drill and ¼" (6-mm) bit
- carpenter's wood glue
- stain or clear wood sealer
- ¼ yd. (22.9 cm) lycra or other stretchy fabric
- old leather glove
- polyester fiberfill
- black electrical tape
- purchased doll boots
- 18-gauge wire
- purchased doll head
- recycled fur
- wool fabric remnants
- glue gun

INSTRUCTIONS

1 ▪ Begin by constructing an armature
using the two dowels and a flat wooden
disk or other base (*fig. 1*). About 1½" to 2"
(3.8 to 5.1 cm) down from the top of the
longer dowel, drill a hole to accommodate
the shorter one. The shorter dowel will form
the shoulders. Drill a hole in the wooden base
to hold the vertical dowel; then secure it in
place with carpenter's glue, allowing the
glue to dry for 24 hours. Remove and set
aside the shoulder dowel for now. Finish
the base, if desired, with stain or clear sealer.

2 ▪ Using the stretchy fabric, construct a
body form about 5" (12.7 cm) in diameter and 9" tall (22.9 cm), leaving both ends
open as shown in *figure 2*. Then cut eight rectangular pieces 1½" by 4½" (3.8 x 11.4 cm) for
arms and legs. Seam and turn right sides out.

3 ▪ Stuff the body, legs, and arms with
polyester fiberfill. Then thread the body
onto the vertical dowel and add more stuffing to make a rounded chest and stomach.

4 ▪ Secure the shoulder dowel in place with
carpenter's glue. After allowing the glue
to dry, pull the top edges of the body casing
up over the shoulders and hand-stitch them
together to anchor the body onto the armature.

5 ▪ Insert the legs into the boots and secure
them with a few turns of electrical tape.
Sew the legs onto the body, making sure the
boots rest solidly on the wooden base.

6 ▪ Cut two of the fingertips from the
leather glove to use as hands. Then cut
a piece of wire about 20" (50.8 cm) long and
thread the fabric arms onto each end. Fold
over each end of the wire into a loop, place
a leather fingertip over the loop, and secure
it to the fabric arm with several turns of electrical tape (*fig. 3*). Twist the center of the wire
around the neck portion of the vertical
dowel and wind each end once around the
shoulder ends of the cross piece.

7 ▪ Make the gown by cutting two pieces
of wool according to the pattern in
figure 4. Seam the sides and sleeves; then
press under a ½" (1.3-cm) hem on the bottom and sleeves. After turning it right side
out, thread the gown onto the figure. If
necessary, add more stuffing to round out
the shape as desired. Tack the hems by hand
or use a glue gun.

8 ▪ Hot-glue the purchased doll head onto
the dowel and pull the neck of the
gown up and around the head.

9 ▪ Cut a collar and cape (*fig. 5*) and hem
them both. Using the glue gun, attach
these around the neck of the figure.

10 ▪ Using strips of old fur, bits of ribbon, and other treasures, personalize your figure as desired. Simply hot-glue
the embellishments in place.

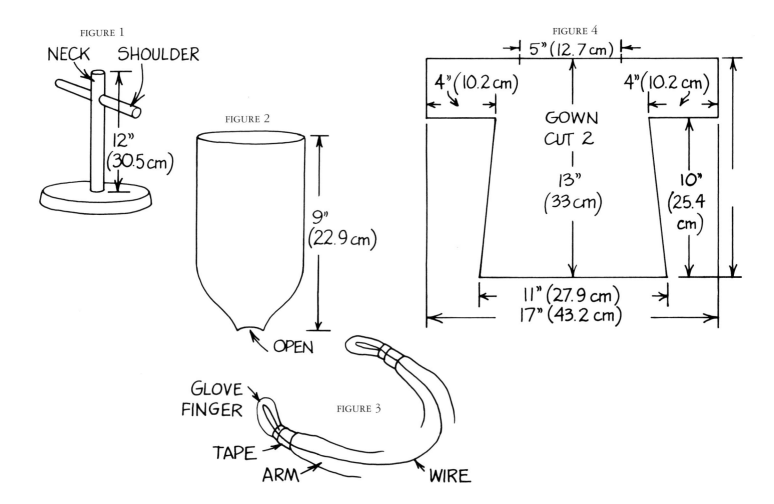

FIGURE 1

NECK   SHOULDER

12"
(30.5 cm)

FIGURE 2

9"
(22.9 cm)

OPEN

GLOVE
FINGER

FIGURE 3

TAPE

ARM   WIRE

FIGURE 4

5" (12.7 cm)

4" (10.2 cm)   4" (10.2 cm)

GOWN
CUT 2

13"
(33 cm)

10"
(25.4
cm)

11" (27.9 cm)
17" (43.2 cm)

FIGURE 5

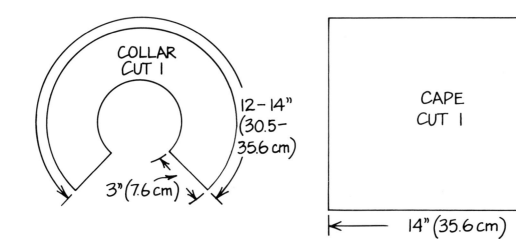

COLLAR
CUT 1

12−14"
(30.5−
35.6 cm)

3" (7.6 cm)

CAPE
CUT 1

11"
(27.9 cm)

14" (35.6 cm)

PAPER & PAPIER-MÂCHÉ

![G] OLFING SANTA

Papier-mâché artist Mary Beth Ruby knows that even Santa needs a break from his routine once in a while. After a year of making toys and a long night of chimney-hopping, what could be more relaxing than knocking around some golf balls?

DESIGN: MARY BETH RUBY
SIZE: 21" (53.3 CM) TALL

MATERIALS & TOOLS

- plastic-coated wire (clothesline or other sturdy yet bendable wire)
- wire cutter
- masking tape
- newspaper
- instant papier-mâché
- plastic wrap
- rolling pin
- craft knife
- small modeling tool
- acrylic paints
- artist's brushes
- acrylic matte varnish
- lamb's wool or artificial fur
- craft glue

INSTRUCTIONS

1 • Form the wire into an armature as shown in *figure 1*. Make a small loop for the head and longer, flattened ones for the arms and legs.

2 • Tear single sheets of newspaper into 3"-wide (7.6 cm) strips and wrap these tightly around the wire armature, securing the newspaper with masking tape. Continue adding strips of paper to build up the form almost as large as you want your Santa.

3 • Position the armature by bending the arms and legs into a golfing posture—a friend or spouse makes a handy model. Cut a short length of wire for the golf club and bend the hands over it to attach it.

4 • Mix the instant papier-mâché according to the instructions on the package. Then place a tennis ball–sized portion of the pulp between two sheets of plastic wrap and flatten it with the rolling pin, making a sheet about ¼" (6 mm) thick. Before handling the pulp, dampen your fingers. Then cover the padded armature with the sheet of papier-mâché. Lay the figure on a sheet of plastic wrap and allow it to dry, turning occasionally.

5 • Once the figure is dry, you'll have a sturdy surface on which to model the features. Don't worry about lumps or cracks; these will be covered by additional layers. Flatten more sheets of pulp and cut pieces to form the boots, front of the jacket, and sleeves. While you're working on the front, lay Santa on his back to dry. Then reverse the process.

6 • For Santa's bag, cut a sheet of pulp into the shape shown in *figure 2*. Curve the sheet into the appropriate shape and attach it to the back of the figure. To hold the bag open, place a wad of foil inside until it dries.

7 • Use small pieces of pulp to create the facial features, modeling them with your fingers and a small tool. To make a smooth finish, dip the tool in water first.

8 • After the figure has dried completely, paint it with acrylic paints and seal it with a coat of varnish. Don't paint where you plan to attach the furry beard; the glue adheres better to unfinished pulp.

9 • Use craft glue to attach the hair and beard to the figure. Place a light coating of glue on the pulp and on the back of the wool; then press firmly to get good adhesion. Fluff out the beard for its full effect.

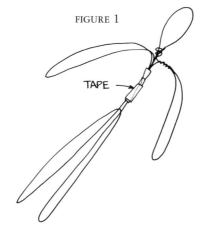

FIGURE 1

TAPE →

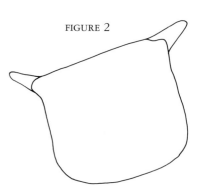

FIGURE 2

FATHER CHRISTMAS WITH TOYS APLENTY

This remarkably impressive figure created by Lorraine Gouge looks as if he's been captured in midsentence. One hand gestures casually, while the other steadies his overflowing bag of toys and presents.

MATERIALS & TOOLS

- wooden base 1½" x 6" x 6" (3.8 x 15.2 x 15.2 cm)
- piece of small-gauge chicken wire, approx. 16" (40.6 cm) square
- needle-nose pliers
- wire cutters
- screwdriver
- 1" (2.5-cm) wood screw with large head
- 8" (20.3 cm) coat hanger wire
- masking tape
- cellulose wallpaper paste
- 100 sheets tissue paper
- 12 sheets typing paper
- brown paper grocery bag
- metal nail file or small sculpting tool
- toothpicks
- instant papier-mâché
- gesso
- lightweight poster board
- artist's brushes
- acrylic paints in colors of your choice
- acrylic matte medium
- 4" (10.2 cm) 21-gauge floral wire
- small piece of clear acetate
- white glue

DESIGN: LORRAINE GOUGE
SIZE: 16" (40.6 CM) TALL, INCLUDING BASE

INSTRUCTIONS

1 ▪ Crush the chicken wire into the general shape of an armless human figure about 11" (27.9 cm) tall (*fig. 1*). Use the wire cutters to snip away excess wire and divide the lower portion into two legs. The papier-mâché will add ¼" (6 mm) or more padding to every surface, so make your armature smaller than you want your figure to be.

2 ▪ Flatten 1" (2.5 cm) of wire at the end of each leg and turn it up to form a foot. Anchor the armature to the base with the wood screw as shown in *figure 1*.

3 ▪ Thread the hanger wire through the shoulders of the armature to form arms. Using the pliers, bend back the ends of the wire to make palms for the hands. Secure the arms into the desired positions with masking tape.

4 ▪ Sprinkle 1 rounded tablespoon (15 ml) of wallpaper paste into 3 cups (710 ml) of cool water. Mix well and let stand at least 20 minutes to thicken. All of the paper you use—except the instant papier-mâché—is to be saturated with this paste before it's applied.

5 ▪ Tear several sheets of typing paper lengthwise into ¾" (1.9-cm) strips and set aside. Then begin tearing tissue paper into irregular pieces about 5" (12.7 cm) square.

6 ▪ Wet strips of typing paper with the paste. After removing excess paste with your fingers, begin covering the armature with the strips. Wrap every surface, including the arms, with at least one layer of paper.

7 ▪ Open a short slit inside one thigh to speed the drying process. Keep the slit open until the figure is completely dry; you can fill it later or simply hide it with the coat.

8 ▪ Moisten your fingers with paste and pick up several pieces of tissue paper. Lightly press the tissue into a small pad, moistening it throughout with paste, and press it onto the head of the figure. Continue adding pads of tissue, building out the head, body, and arms until they are in proportion. Sculpt the face with your small tools and shape the palms of the hands (fingers will be added later).

9 ▪ Now is a good time to let your figure dry for a day or two. You may pause at any stage and let it dry; just be sure to moisten the surface when you begin again.

10 ▪ When your figure is dry, make these measurements: top of shoulder to wrist, across back from shoulder to shoulder, back of neck to waist, around waist, from waist to desired bottom of coat. Using these measurements for size, sketch the clothing shown in *figure 2* onto typing paper and that in *figure 3* onto brown paper. If in doubt, cut the pieces slightly larger; you can always trim them later.

11 ▪ Moisten one sleeve with paste, removing the excess with your fingers. Turn under the lower edge, overlap the underarm seam, and press the edges together. Slip the sleeve over the arm and press it into place. Repeat with the other sleeve and coat pieces. Gather the extra fullness at the waist and press it in place.

12 ▪ Place a small pad of tissue on one half of the pouch. Fold in the edges and press the two halves together. Paste the pouch to the waist, leaving the top third loose. Cover the waist seam with the belt and press the pouch flap down over the belt. Add the buckle.

13 ▪ Flare the coat at the bottom and use toothpicks to hold it away from the legs until it stiffens.

14 ▪ Add the hair, beard, and mustache by forming small rolls of tissue. Fold under the edge of the hat, roll it into a cone, and press it onto the head. Then fold down the tip.

15 ▪ Fold up the lower edges of the gloves. Place matching halves onto the palms and press the fingers together. Join the outside edges to form a cuff. When the fingers have dried, you may trim them with scissors.

16 ▪ Wrap the boot tops around the legs from just below the knees to the base. Add the toe pieces and fill in with extra bits of brown paper to form boots.

17 ▪ Shape the toy bag and arrange it so that one hand grips the edge. Lightly stuff the bottom of the bag with crumpled typing paper.

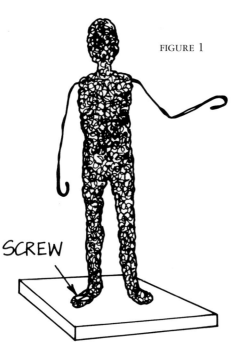

FIGURE 1

SCREW

18. Following the instructions on the package, mix a small amount of instant papier-mâché for the fur trim. Moisten the appropriate areas with paste and apply the "fur" with your fingers or small tool.

19. After covering the base with moist tissue to look like snow, let your figure dry thoroughly.

20. In the meantime, make some toys for the bag—a drum, doll, teddy bear, gift box—using poster board, tissue, typing paper, and instant papier-mâché.

21. Coat your entire figure, including the bag and snow-covered base, and all toys with gesso. Once dry, paint your figure and toys with acrylic paints, using the colors of your choice. To protect the surface, apply a coat of matte medium.

22. Using pliers, shape a piece of floral wire into spectacles. Cut small pieces of clear plastic for lenses and glue them in place. Then glue the spectacles onto Santa's nose.

FIGURE 2

FIGURE 3

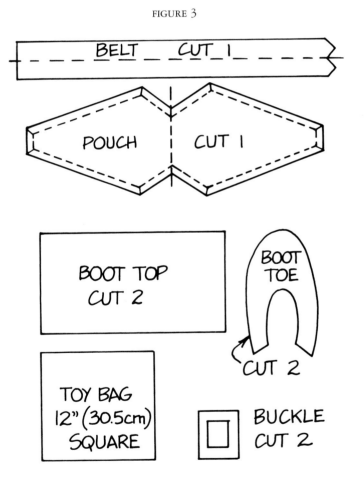

JINGLE BELL TRIO

This divine trio of Santas is the creation of Virginia Boegli, who has devised an unusual form of papier-mâché. She obtains the smooth, glassy surface by employing paper towels for the mâché and translucent washes of color for her paints.

DESIGN: VIRGINIA BOEGLI
SIZE: 8½" (21.6 CM) TALL

MATERIALS & TOOLS

- aluminum foil
- cellulose wallpaper paste
- white glue
- 1" (2.5-cm) paste brush
- sheet of glass or plastic at least 10" x 14" (25.4 x 35.6 cm)
- plain white paper towels
- metal drying rack
- coat hanger wire
- wire cutters
- scrap piece of wood 1" x 4" x 4" (2.5 x 10.2 x 10.2 cm)
- electric drill and assorted bits
- small watercolor brushes
- acrylic paints

INSTRUCTIONS

1. Make an armature by cutting four strips of aluminum foil—two 9" x 12" (22.9 x 30.5 cm) and two 6" x 16" (15.2 x 40.6 cm). Shape the first 9" x 12" piece into a head and torso and the second into the legs and feet (*fig. 1*). Use one 6" x 16" strip to make the arms and hands (*fig. 2*) and the second one to make a belly (*fig. 3*).

2. To make the paste, mix three parts of prepared cellulose paste with one part white glue.

3. A combination of paper towels and paste forms the mâché. Using the larger brush, liberally coat the glass palette with paste. Lay one paper towel on the palette and coat it with a layer of paste. Place another towel on top of the first, matching the edges, and coat it with paste as well. This is your mâché.

4. Starting at one serrated edge, tear off a strip of mâché and begin covering the armature. Starting behind the left shoulder, pass the strip down across the body and finish by wrapping the right leg (*fig. 4*). Repeat with the other side and continue with pieces of mâché until the armature is covered.

5. Set the figure on the wire rack to dry thoroughly.

6. Build a temporary support to hold the figure in a standing position while you work on him. Using heavy coat hanger wire, cut a straight piece 6" to 8" (15.2 to 20.3 cm) long. Choose a drill bit the same size as the wire and drill a hole not quite all the way through the center of the scrap of wood. Insert the wire into the hole.

7. Place the figure on the support (*fig. 5*) and continue to flesh out the body with strips of mâché. Then set it aside to dry overnight.

8. The following day, arrange Santa in the desired pose (*fig. 6*). If necessary, moisten the figure with warm water to make him more pliable. Wet the figure briefly and allow the moisture to penetrate for a few minutes before making the adjustments. Using larger pieces of mâché, fashion Santa's clothing.

9. After the figure has dried overnight, remove Santa from the support and check to see if he stands on his own. If he's unsteady, make another batch of mâché and build up his feet until he stands on his own. Discard any unused mâché and let Santa dry overnight.

10. Using the larger brush, coat Santa with paste, working it into all the crevices. Allow the paste to dry.

11. Starting with the face, paint the features with acrylic paint thinned to a translucent wash. Continue painting the clothing until you are satisfied with the results. If desired, add a coat of glossy acrylic varnish to the dry painted surface.

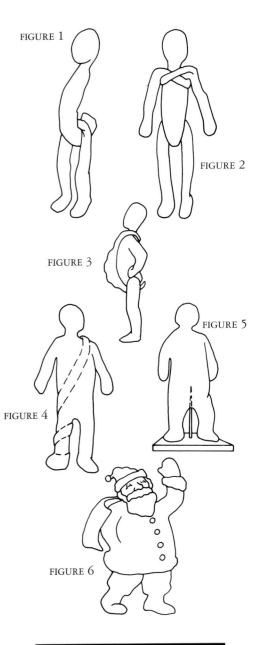

FIGURE 1

FIGURE 2

FIGURE 3

FIGURE 5

FIGURE 4

FIGURE 6

ANDMADE PAPER SANTA PLAQUES

To make her colorful handmade paper without adding dyes or other chemicals, Claudia Lee collects flyers, junk mail, office throw-aways, and brochures. The whimsical figures that result can be made any size you like, from small Christmas tree ornaments to large wall or door decorations.

DESIGN: CLAUDIA LEE
SIZES: FROM 10" TO 16" (25.4 TO 40.6 CM) TALL

MATERIALS & TOOLS

- assorted good-quality papers
- blender
- strainer or colander
- containers to hold pulp (one for each color)
- piece of high-quality medium-weight interfacing
- sponge
- fiberglass screening
- puff paints

INSTRUCTIONS

1 ▪ When making your paper, don't use too much glossy paper, such as magazine pages, and be sure to remove any staples or plastic. Sort the papers into color families to keep the colors bright. If you combine unlike colors, you will get a muddy gray. If you're recycling all white papers, you can make them different colors by adding pieces of construction paper to the mix.

2 ▪ Tear the papers into small pieces about the size of a large coin and soak them well in water. After filling the blender three-quarters full of water, add a handful of the soaked pieces. Make sure the lid is on tight! Using short bursts, turn on the blender. If it sounds as though the motor is straining, stop the blender, remove some of the pulp, and add more water. Process again.

3 ▪ When the pulp is as smooth as oatmeal or finer, it's done. Pour it through a strainer and into a container. Repeat this process until you have enough pulp for your project. Process and collect each color separately.

4 ▪ Cut a piece of interfacing a bit larger than your Santa will be. If desired, sketch an outline of the desired pose, or plan to work freehand with the pulp. Immerse the fabric in water and squeeze out the excess. Then smooth out the wrinkles and spread the fabric on a flat surface.

5 ▪ Begin by placing a small handful of wet pulp (don't squeeze out the water) where you want it on the fabric. Form, manipulate, and move the pulp around until you're satisfied with how it looks. Whenever you add another color, be sure to overlap it a bit with the rest of the piece so that it will bond together.

6 ▪ When you're satisfied with your Santa, place a piece of fiberglass screen on top and apply steady pressure with your sponge, squeezing out as much water as you can. This helps bond the fibers and diminishes shrinkage. Set the piece aside to dry thoroughly.

7 ▪ When your Santa is completely dry, remove the interfacing.

8 ▪ You may notice that the colors become softer and more muted as the paper dries. If you want to restore the darker tones, brush melted paraffin on both sides of the piece. Take great care when melting wax; it's extremely flammable. Using an old Crockpot is a safe method. After liberally coating the piece with paraffin, set it on several layers of newspaper. Place this on a cookie sheet and bake it in a 250°F (120°C) oven for about five minutes or until the wax has melted into the paper.

9 ▪ Using puff paints and other embellishments, complete your Santa by adding facial features, clothing details, and textures. Add a hanger, if desired, by hot-gluing a loop of wire or cord to the back of your piece.

MERRY MR. CLAUS

In her work with papier-mâché, Lorraine Gouge is a master of subtle detail; even her simplest figures display remarkable personalities.

This jolly fellow looks as though he's just about to burst into a medley of his favorite Christmas carols.

DESIGN: LORRAINE GOUGE
SIZE: 8" (20.3 CM) TALL

MATERIALS & TOOLS

- aluminum foil
- needle-nose pliers
- masking tape
- cellulose wallpaper paste
- 30–40 sheets white tissue paper
- metal nail file or small sculpting tool
- 4 sheets typing paper
- heavy brown paper grocery bag
- instant papier-mâché
- toothpicks
- heavy cardboard 3" or 4" (7.6 or 10.2 cm) square
- gesso
- artist's brushes
- acrylic paints
- acrylic matte medium
- white glue
- wire cutters
- 21-gauge floral wire
- small piece of clear acetate

INSTRUCTIONS

1 ▪ To make an armature, crush a piece of foil 12" x 18" (30.5 x 45.7 cm) into a firm roll 6" (15.2 cm) long. Repeat with a second piece of foil. Turn up enough at the bottom of each roll to make a 1" (2.5 cm) foot. Round the toes, flatten the bottoms of the feet, and shape the lower legs with the pliers. Squeeze a third piece of foil 12" (30.5 cm) square into an oval ball about 1½" (3.8 cm) long for the head, leaving a 1½" tab of foil at the bottom.

2 ▪ Assemble the armature by placing the head on top of the two rolls of foil, with the tab between the rolls to anchor the head in place (*fig. 1*). Tape the rolls together to form a body with short legs.

3 ▪ Sprinkle 1 rounded tablespoon (15 ml) of wallpaper paste into 3 cups (710 ml) of cool water. Mix well and let stand for 20 minutes to thicken. Use this paste to saturate all of the paper you apply to your figure.

4 ▪ Tear the tissue paper into irregular pieces about 5" (12.7 cm) square and place them in a flat container for easy access. After coating your fingers with paste, pick up several pieces of tissue. Shape the wet tissue into a pad and press it onto the head of the figure.

5 ▪ Keep adding pads of tissue to shape the head, body, legs, and feet. After filling out the shoulders, form the arms and hands against the body. Each hand is a slightly flattened ball of tissue with a thumb added at the top.

6 ▪ Sculpt the face with your tools, but don't add the long hair and beard until the figure is dressed. Then allow the figure to dry for a day or more.

7 ▪ Measure the figure to determine the size and accessories you'll need. Using *figure 2* as a guide, sketch the clothing pieces on typing paper. Use *figure 3* to sketch the boots and other accessories on brown paper. Then draw the soles on a piece of cardboard. Cut all the pieces.

8 ▪ Starting with the boots, immerse each piece into the paste and wipe off any excess with your fingers. Wrap a boot top around each leg, joining the edges to make a seam down the back. Make a small cut in front to fit this piece over the sides of the foot. Fold in the bottom edges and tuck them under the heel. Apply the boot toes, tucking under those edges also. Wherever needed, fill in with bits of brown paper. You will glue on the boot soles when your figure is dry.

9 ▪ Using the photo as a guide, fit the other clothing pieces over the figure and press them in place. Use extra bits of typing paper to fill any gaps. Lap the coat and cover the seam at the waist with the belt and buckle.

10 ▪ Make the hair and beard with tiny rolls and strands of moist tissue, arranging them with your tools.

11 ▪ After coating it with paste, shape the brown paper rectangle into a sack. Fill the sack with some crumpled typing paper; then arrange it over Santa's shoulder, tucking the ends under the thumbs and tops of the hands. Gather the sack neck piece and tuck it under the bottoms of the hands so that it appears Santa is grasping the sack in his hands.

12 ▪ After turning under the bottom edge, form the hat by rolling it into a cone. Then place it on the head and fold down the point. Add a sprig of paper holly for decoration.

13 ▪ Mix about ½ cup (118 ml) of instant papier-mâché, following the instructions on the package. Use this to make the fur trim on the coat and hat. Moisten the areas to be trimmed; then apply the fur with your fingers or a small tool. Use a toothpick to roughen the surface and make it look furry.

14 ▪ Allow your figure to dry thoroughly. This may take a week or more. When it's completely dry, glue on the boot soles.

15 ▪ Using a medium-sized brush, coat the entire figure and sack with gesso. In an hour or so the figure will be ready to paint. Paint the figure in the colors of your choice. When it's dry, apply a coat of acrylic matte medium to protect the surface.

16 ▪ Shape the floral wire into half-round spectacles with the pliers. For lenses, cut half-circles of clear acetate and glue them into the frames. Then glue the spectacles in place on Santa's nose.

FIGURE 1

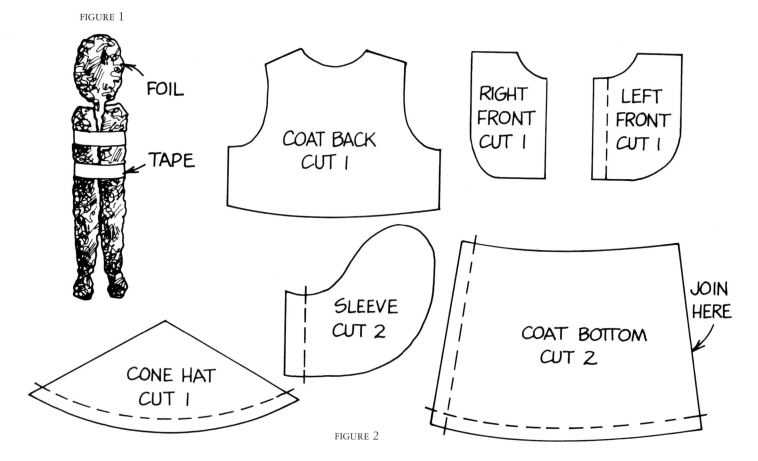

FOIL

TAPE

COAT BACK
CUT 1

RIGHT
FRONT
CUT 1

LEFT
FRONT
CUT 1

SLEEVE
CUT 2

JOIN
HERE

COAT BOTTOM
CUT 2

CONE HAT
CUT 1

FIGURE 2

FIGURE 3

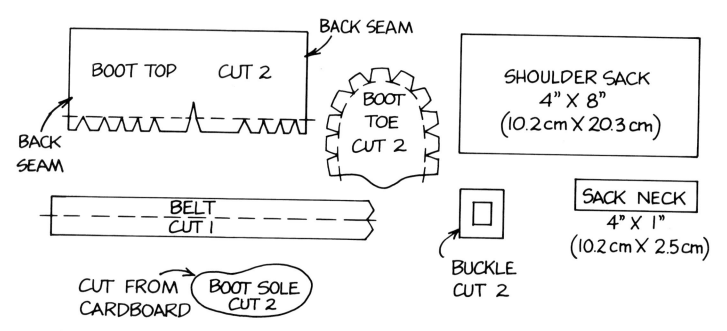

BACK SEAM

BOOT TOP   CUT 2

BACK
SEAM

BOOT
TOE
CUT 2

SHOULDER SACK
4" X 8"
(10.2 cm X 20.3 cm)

BELT
CUT 1

CUT FROM
CARDBOARD

BOOT SOLE
CUT 2

BUCKLE
CUT 2

SACK NECK
4" X 1"
(10.2 cm X 2.5 cm)

VICTORIAN FATHER CHRISTMAS

Our Victorian-Era forebears had a tendency to take their holidays with a greater degree of seriousness than we do today. Mary Beth Ruby reflects this perspective in a rather dour Santa who's seen perhaps one too many empty stockings awaiting him.

MATERIALS & TOOLS

- instant papier-mâché
- plastic wrap
- rolling pin
- 12" (30.5-cm) polystyrene cone
- craft knife
- modeling tools
- acrylic paints
- artist's brushes
- acrylic matte varnish
- self-stick felt

INSTRUCTIONS

1 • Mix the instant papier-mâché according to the manufacturer's instructions. Place a ball of the pulp between two sheets of plastic wrap and flatten it into a sheet about ⅛" (3 mm) thick with the rolling pin.

2 • After first dampening your fingers, smooth the sheet onto the cone. Then allow it to dry for a day or two.

3 • Flatten additional sheets of papier-mâché and cut them into pieces for the arms, beard, fur trim, and hat. For the facial features and teddy bear, apply small bits of pulp with your damp fingers. Then smooth and refine them with the modeling tool. Using the same tool, make long vertical grooves in the beard and hair. Don't worry about any small cracks and bumps; these will help make your figure look more like an antique.

4 • After the papier-mâché has dried completely, paint your Santa with acrylic paints. To dull the bright acrylic colors and give your figure an antique appearance, apply a thin coating of well-diluted burnt umber acrylic paint. Before it dries, wipe off the excess paint with a rag or paper towel. Seal the painted surface with a coat of acrylic varnish.

5 • Cover the bottom of the cone with a circle of self-stick felt.

DESIGN: MARY BETH RUBY
SIZE: 13" (33 CM) TALL

TALL SANTA BEARING GIFTS

With the simplest of tools—some acrylic paints and a short length of pine—Guy Koppi has created an heirloom Santa to hang on the wall or display on the mantel. This Santa makes an excellent family project; even very young children can apply the gesso and base colors, leaving the detail work for the more skilled "artists" in the family.

DESIGN: GUY KOPPI
SIZE: 2½" x 23" (6.4 x 58.4 CM)

MATERIALS & TOOLS

- white pine board ⅝" x 2½" x 24" (1.6 x 6.4 x 61 cm)
- tracing pen or soft pencil
- jigsaw
- medium and fine sandpaper
- acrylic gesso
- acrylic paints
- artist's brushes
- satin polyurethane
- small picture-hanging bracket
- carpenter's wood glue (freestanding Santa only)

INSTRUCTIONS

1 ▪ Trace or sketch the pattern in *figure 1* on one end of the pine board. Cut as indicated, saving the scrap to make a stand if desired. Using medium-grit sandpaper, sand all of the edges until they're smooth.

2 ▪ Apply two coats of gesso to every surface, including the reserved piece, and allow it to dry between applications. Sand after each coat with fine sandpaper, paying particular attention to the front surface.

3 ▪ Mix some red paint with a little yellow and black to use for the hat. Brush a deep green color onto the lower two-thirds of the figure for the coat. Darken each base color slightly with a little black paint, brushing lightly over the painted areas for an antiquing effect. Paint in the darkened area of the hat to suggest a fold in the fabric. Mix your preferred skin tone and apply it to the face area.

4 ▪ After the main color areas have dried, transfer the detail patterns (*fig. 2*) to the figure. The line of the mouth should be located about 8½" (21.6 cm) from the top.

5 ▪ Starting with the easier ones, begin painting the details. Mix and apply a grey tone to the bell. Then add darker shadows and white highlights as shown in the photograph.

6 ▪ Paint the front of the package with the desired color. Darken the color with a little black and apply this to the right side of the box. Add a little more black for the top. When this is dry, use a contrasting color for the bow, mixing in some white for highlights.

7 ▪ Paint mittens over the bottom of the box and apply highlights with a stiff brush and a stippling motion, or use a sponge to give them a textured appearance. Mix the green with a little white and brush upward from the mittens to the sides of the figure to suggest sleeves.

8 ▪ Begin the face by using a liner brush and black paint to draw the outline of the eyes, nose, and mouth. Fill in the eye color, adding black to the center and two dabs of white in each eye for highlights. Mix the skin tone again and darken it slightly to apply around the eyes, nose, and mouth (*fig. 3*). Cover the black almost completely, leaving just enough to define the features. Finish the eyes and mouth.

9 ▪ Complete the painting by applying white for the brim of the hat, eyebrows, beard, and piping on the coat. Use gesso for a more textured effect in these areas. For the beard, pull the paint downward into the coat for a feathered effect. Using the same technique, suggest hair under the brim of the hat and at the sides of the face. Allow the paint to dry overnight.

10 ▪ For a freestanding Santa, glue the reserved piece of wood to the bottom of the back and allow it to dry. Apply polyurethane to the back. When the back is dry, apply a generous coat of polyurethane to the front and sides. If you plan to use your Santa as a wall or door ornament, affix a hanger bracket to the upper back of the figure once the finish is completely dry.

PAINTED IMAGES

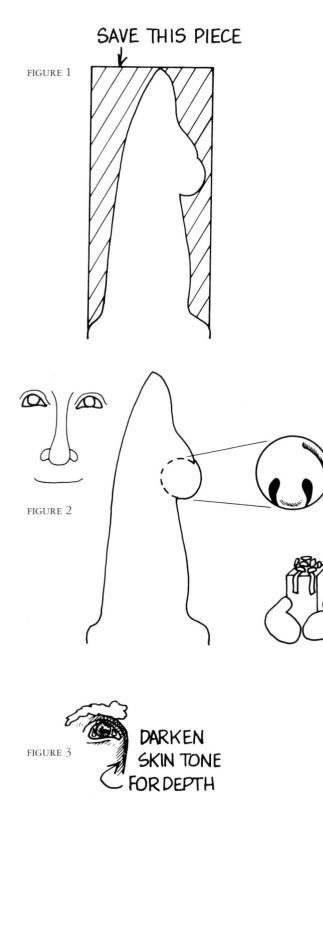

FIGURE 1

SAVE THIS PIECE

FIGURE 2

FIGURE 3 DARKEN SKIN TONE FOR DEPTH

OON & STARS SANTA

Lively sparkling eyes and rich textures distinguish the images on Susan Forrest's painted gourds. Santa's exuberant hair and beard look wind-tossed, and his rosy cheeks indicate he has just come inside from a long, cold journey around the globe.

MATERIALS & TOOLS

- hard-shell gourd, cured and cleaned
- sandpaper
- red or blue latex paint
- water-based satin varnish
- flat brushes
- artist's brushes
- artist's oil paints in several colors

DESIGN: SUSAN FORREST
SIZE: 8½" x 13" (21.6 x 33 CM)

INSTRUCTIONS

1 ▪ Using latex paint in the color most prominent in your design, apply a base coat to the gourd. Allow it to dry completely.

2 ▪ Complete the preparation of your gourd by applying a coat of satin varnish. This assures a smooth working surface and enables you to make corrections to your painting.

3 ▪ Use *figure 1* or photographs of family or friends as a guide for painting the face of your Santa. Susan Forrest paints freehand, but you may wish to transfer the figure or sketch a design on the gourd to guide you. For best results, continue your design around the back with sufficient detail to make it interesting.

4 ▪ You will be much happier with the results if you choose quality brushes and paints for your project. Use flat brushes for broad areas of color and rounded artist's brushes for details. If you're not an experienced painter, don't be discouraged if your first attempt isn't worthy of museum display. Experiment by blending colors as you paint to give more depth to your design. Oil paint dries much more slowly than acrylic, and you can easily work two or more colors together for smooth transitions. Pay careful attention to the eyes, noting the highlight in each pupil and the shading of the iris.

5 ▪ Once your design is complete, allow the oil paint to dry thoroughly. This may take a week or more.

6 ▪ To seal the gourd and protect the painting, apply several coats of satin varnish. Water-based varnish dries quickly, and more than one coat can be applied in a day. Five or more coats are recommended if you want your gourd to last a lifetime.

FIGURE 1

POTATO PRINT CARD HOLDER

Although raw potatoes may appear to be unlikely tools for printmaking, both adults and children find them easy to carve and use. Fleta Monaghan designed and executed the larger card holder; her eight-year-old daughter, Mary, created and printed the design for the smaller one.

DESIGN: FLETA MONAGHAN
SIZE: 12½" x 19" (31.8 x 48.3 CM)
AND 12½" x 11½" (31.8 x 29.2 CM)

MATERIALS & TOOLS

- ½ yd. (45.7 cm) firm red fabric
- ½ yd. (45.7 cm) firm white fabric
- ¾ yd. (68.6 cm) fusible interfacing
- sewing thread
- sewing machine
- fabric glue
- raw potato
- paring knife
- acrylic paints
- small hollow plastic tube 12" (30.5 cm) long
- 1 yd. (91.4 cm) red ribbon or cord

INSTRUCTIONS

1 • Cut the fabric pieces as indicated in the patterns in *figure 1*. Then cut the interfacing to the finished sizes of the three components: 12½" x 19" (31.8 x 48.3 cm) for the backing, 12½" x 8½" (31.8 x 21.6 cm) for the middle pocket, and 12½" x 9" (31.8 x 22.9 cm) for the bottom pocket.

2 • Center the smaller pieces of interfacing onto the reverse sides of the pocket fabrics, allowing a 1" (2.5-cm) hem all around. Place the third piece of interfacing on the backing so that there is a 1" hem on the sides and bottom only. Following the manufacturer's guidelines, fuse the interfacing to the fabrics.

3 • Turn the top and bottom hems of the two pockets and sew or glue them in place.

4 • Position the middle pocket onto the backing so that the top of the pocket is 6½" (16.5 cm) down from the top of the backing. After pinning it in place, sew across the bottom of the pocket with a ½" (1.3-cm) seam.

5 • Pin the bottom pocket onto the backing so that the bottom edge of the pocket slightly overlaps that of the backing. Now turn both bottom edges together and sew or glue the hem. Make a hem on the right edge by turning the pockets and backing together. Sew or glue the hem; then repeat with the left edge.

6 • Using the 1½" (3.8 cm) of extra fabric at the top edge of the backing, make a casing wide enough to hold your hollow plastic tube. Your card holder is now ready to decorate.

7 • Slice the potato in half lengthwise. Lightly sketch your design (see *figure 2*) onto the cut surface with a marking pen or the point of a paring knife. Using the knife, cut away portions of the potato to leave the Santa image.

8 • Test your design by making some practice prints on scrap fabric. Dip your carved potato into a saucer of paint. You may need to brush away some excess if the paint fills small areas such as the eye sockets, but leave enough paint to make a strong image. Then press firmly onto the fabric.

9 • When you're satisfied with your test prints, use contrasting colors (e.g., white paint on red fabric) to stamp the potato onto the card holder where desired.

10 • Insert the plastic tube into the casing and thread the cord through the tube. You can tie a bow at the top or glue the ends of the cord together and hide the joint in the tube.

FIGURE 1

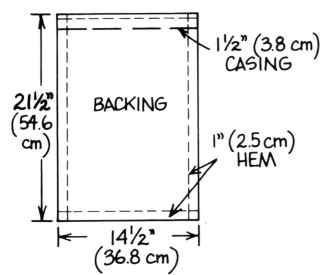

21½"
(54.6 cm)

BACKING

1½" (3.8 cm) CASING

1" (2.5 cm) HEM

14½"
(36.8 cm)

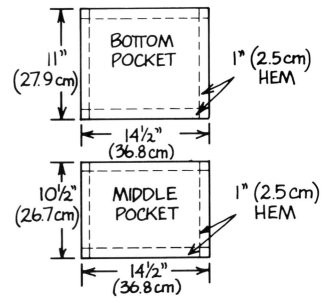

BOTTOM POCKET

11"
(27.9 cm)

1" (2.5cm) HEM

14½"
(36.8 cm)

MIDDLE POCKET

10½"
(26.7cm)

1" (2.5 cm) HEM

14½"
(36.8 cm)

FIGURE 2

CHESTNUT SNAG SANTA

Bonnie Bullman fashions her folk-art Santas from the remnants of great chestnut trees that once stood tall in the forests near her home. When you're out in the woods scouting materials, look for interesting shapes on any downed tree that has been weathered by wind and rain.

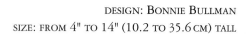

DESIGN: BONNIE BULLMAN
SIZE: FROM 4" TO 14" (10.2 TO 35.6 CM) TALL

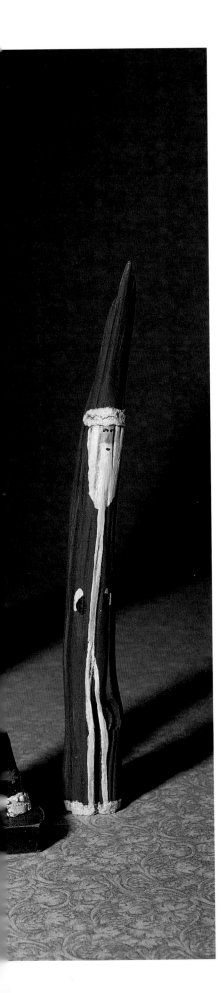

MATERIALS & TOOLS

- wood snag
- jigsaw or handsaw
- sandpaper
- acrylic paints
- small paintbrush
- textured snow medium
- matte acrylic spray sealer
- brown antiquing stain
- small pine board
- carpenter's wood glue
- wooden stars or sprigs of berries or herbs

INSTRUCTIONS

1 ▪ Saw the bottom of the wood snag to make it flat; then sand all the surfaces with the grain of the wood until they're smooth. Wipe off any sawdust or dirt with a damp rag.

2 ▪ Using acrylic paint in the color you wish for the robe, paint the entire surface of the snag.

3 ▪ When the base coat is dry, paint an oval in the face area using the desired skin tone. Allow it to dry.

4 ▪ Using white paint, add hair and a beard; then paint a pair of mittens with black. Facial features can be suggested with black eyes, a brown nose, and a red mouth (*fig. 1*). The size and texture of the snag usually won't allow you to include much detail, and the desired effect is one of simplicity not sophistication.

5 ▪ Using textured snow medium, paint the fur trim on Santa's hat, coat, and sleeves.

6 ▪ When the surface is completely dry, apply a coat of acrylic sealer. Allow this to dry thoroughly.

7 ▪ Apply the brown antiquing stain and immediately wipe off the excess. Leave enough to darken the bright acrylic colors but not obscure them. The stain will remain in the cracks, emphasizing the grain of the wood and making the piece look aged.

8 ▪ Protect the painted surface by sealing it with acrylic spray.

9 ▪ To make a stand for your Santa, cut an appropriate shape from the pine board. Sand all the edges and paint it black. When the paint is dry, apply a coat of matte acrylic spray. Lightly sand the edges and apply antiquing stain. Wipe off the excess and allow it to dry. Then seal it with acrylic spray.

10 ▪ Attach the snag to the stand with carpenter's wood glue. If desired, attach wooden stars or sprigs of berries or herbs as decorations.

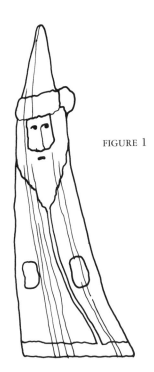

FIGURE 1

PAINTED EGG ORNAMENTS

Pat Scheible creates family heirlooms from all types of eggs—chicken, cockatoo, goose, or quail. The outside surfaces are hand painted, and the insides contain tiny dioramas with festive themes.

DESIGN: PAT SCHEIBLE

SIZES: BROWN, 2½" x 4"
(6.4 x 10.2 CM);
BLUE, 1¾" x 2¾"
(4.4 x 7 CM)

MATERIALS & TOOLS

- infertile egg of your choice
- needle
- fine manicure scissors or motorized "mini-tool"
- lighted magnifying glass
- acrylic paints
- artist's brushes
- onion skins, white and purple
- stylus with sharp point
- spray matte acrylic sealer
- German N-gauge model railroad figurines
- white glue
- decorative ribbon trim
- pendant finding

INSTRUCTIONS

1 ▪ Pierce the ends of the egg with a needle and blow out the contents.

2 ▪ If you want to make a diorama, you must soften the shell before cutting it. Soak the shell in water overnight; then cut an oval hole in one side with the manicure scissors or "mini-tool."

3 ▪ Begin your diorama by painting the background image. The area is small and fragile, so you won't be able to make a sketch. Using a lighted magnifying glass to help you see, paint the area with a fine artist's brush and acrylic paints.

4 ▪ Paint the miniature figurines with the colors of your choice. Then set these aside until you finish with the outside of the shell.

5 ▪ Transfer one of the designs in *figure 1* or create a new image by sketching very lightly on the shell with a soft pencil. Add paint in blocks of color, starting with the main figure and finishing with smaller details.

6 ▪ If you want to make a reverse image like that on the brown egg, first boil the egg with a generous quantity of onion skins for about 2 hours. A light chalk outline of your figure may be useful, but it's likely to smudge as you work. Using a sharp stylus, gently scratch the image in a series of small strokes. The closer you place your scratches, the lighter the area will become. This is the opposite effect of normal drawing, so you may want to try it on a few practice eggs first.

7 ▪ Once your scratched image is complete, spray the entire outside surface of the egg with two or three coats of clear matte sealer.

8 ▪ Now complete your diorama by installing the figurines and other items, such as trees made from stems of herbs, paper buildings, or cotton snow. Tiny dabs of white glue are sufficient to hold them in place.

9 ▪ Hide the cut edge by gluing a piece of ribbon trim around the opening.

10 ▪ Finish your ornament by gluing a pendant finding onto the top of the egg.

FIGURE 1

LIGHT-OF-THE-MOON JACKET

Pat Scheible is an artist of many talents but is probably best known for her exceptional jackets. Some are handmade from scratch, but many—including this one—are thrift store finds that are transformed by her creativity into works of art.

MATERIALS & TOOLS

- jacket with relatively smooth surface
- newspaper
- short-term spray adhesive
- sharp scissors
- light gray metallic auto touch-up spray paint
- assorted acrylic fabric paints in squeeze bottles
- star-shaped sequins in various sizes
- white glue

INSTRUCTIONS

1 ▪ Cut a hole 10" (25.4 cm) in diameter in a piece of newspaper. Lightly spray the newspaper with a temporary-bond adhesive and press it firmly in place on the back of the jacket.

2 ▪ Enlarge the silhouette of Santa and his reindeer (fig. 1) so that it will fit within the moon hole. Carefully cut out the silhouette, retaining as much detail as possible, and spray one side with the adhesive. Press it into place within the moon hole.

3 ▪ Mask off the rest of the jacket with additional newspaper. Then lightly spray with paint. Easy does it! A light film of color is more attractive than heavy globs. You can lift the edge of your stencils to check your progress. When you're satisfied with the coverage, remove the newspaper and silhouette.

4 ▪ Using the fabric paints, add trees and Christmas greetings. Enrich the sky with star sequins, adding a dollop of glitter paint to cover the holes in the sequins. For added holiday sparkle, fill the plain jacket buttons with glitter paint and press stars into them.

FIGURE 1

DESIGN: Pat Scheible

WEARABLES

DESIGN: SUSAN FORREST

SIZES: 1½" x 2" (3.8 x 5.1 CM)
AND 1¼" x 1¼" (3.2 x 3.2 CM)

SANTA GOURD PENDANT

Susan Forrest deftly incorporated the individual character of each gourd into these hand-painted pendants. The faces appear so lifelike because she modeled them after friends and family members.

MATERIALS & TOOLS

- tiny ornamental or hard-shell gourd
- sandpaper
- red or blue latex paint
- water-based satin varnish
- 0 and 00 artist's brushes
- assortment of artist's oil paints
- magnifying light
- motorized "mini-tool" or drill with tiny bit
- pendant bail and screw eye
- cyanoacrylate glue

INSTRUCTIONS

1 Tiny gourds are accidents of nature; they occur when plants have been stunted by drought or other conditions. When you find small ones, set aside several to cure because some may be young gourds that were picked prematurely. These will shrivel as they age and can't be used.

2 Once the gourd has cured sufficiently, clean and lightly sand it.

3 Apply a base coat to the entire gourd, using latex paint in the color that will be most dominant in your design.

4 Once the paint has dried, apply a coat of water-based satin varnish. This gives a smoother surface for the brushes and makes it easier to correct mistakes in your painting.

5 Use the oil paints and good quality artist's brushes for the decorative painting. You will have much greater success if you use quality tools. Not even an experienced artist can paint well with a poor brush. A magnifying light will enable you to see and execute detailed features with a very fine brush.

6 To guide your painting, use *figure 1* or other pictures, not necessarily of Santa. Susan Forrest paints her faces from photographs of people she knows. Be sure to continue your painting around the back of the gourd, since it will tend to show when the pendant is worn.

7 It may take a week or longer for the oil paint to dry. When it does, there should be no telltale odor remaining. Once the paint is dry, seal the gourd with several coats of satin varnish. Apply four or five coats to protect your artwork and give the gourd a durable finish.

8 Drill a tiny hole in the top of the gourd to accommodate the peg on the screw eye. Glue this in place with cyanoacrylate glue.

9 Once the glue has dried, apply the pendant bail and slip the pendant onto a chain or cord to wear.

FIGURE 1

PAPIER-MÂCHÉ SANTA PINS

These cheery little pins are among the most popular of Mary Beth Ruby's papier-mâché designs. They require a very small investment of time and materials, yet they provide noteworthy accessories for your holiday wardrobe.

MATERIALS & TOOLS

- instant papier-mâché
- plastic wrap
- rolling pin
- plastic knife
- pin back
- acrylic paints
- artist's brushes
- acrylic gloss varnish

INSTRUCTIONS

1 ▪ Following the instructions on the package, prepare a small quantity of instant papier-mâché. Then place a ball of pulp between two pieces of plastic wrap and use a rolling pin to flatten it into a sheet about ¼" (6 mm) thick.

2 ▪ Dip the plastic knife into water so that it won't stick to the pulp and cut a teardrop shape. Then smooth the edges with dampened fingers. On the back side, attach a pin back by pressing a small dab of pulp over the center of the metal bar.

3 ▪ Place the piece face down on a sheet of plastic wrap and allow it to dry. The following day, turn it over and let it dry from the other side. You can hasten the drying process by placing the pin on a cookie sheet and warming it in an oven set at 250°F (120°C). After 30 minutes, carefully turn it over; then allow the piece to bake another half-hour or until dry, checking its progress frequently.

4 ▪ Using fine brushes and the colors of your choice, paint Santa's face, jacket, hat, and bag full of goodies. (Refer to *figure 1*.) Then seal the painted surface with a coat of varnish.

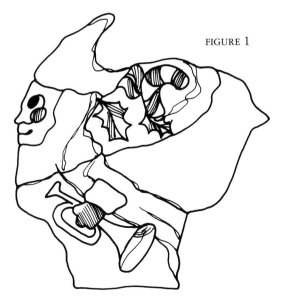

FIGURE 1

DESIGN: MARY BETH RUBY
SIZE: APPROXIMATELY 1½" x 2" (3.8 x 5.1 cm)

DESIGN: GAY SYMMES

SIZES: CHILDREN'S 6–7,
8–10, AND 10–13

SANTA SLIPPER SOCKS

Children of all ages will adore these cozy knitted slippers designed by Gay Symmes. Whether you place Santa at the top or bottom of the design—or one of each as in this pair—they knit up very quickly to make perfect last-minute gifts.

MATERIALS & TOOLS

- 1 skein bright green worsted-weight yarn
- short lengths of red, white, black, and pink yarn
- knitting needles: 1 pair #4, 1 set #4 dp
- markers
- tapestry needle
- cable needle
- bobbins, if desired
- 1 pair commercially made moccasin soles

INSTRUCTIONS

Instructions are for children's shoe sizes 6–7(8–10,10–13) and gauge is 6 sts = 1" (2.5 cm). Center the cable pattern or the Santa graph on the leg of the slippers, adding or subtracting a stitch as needed to keep the design centered. When working from a graph, work from right to left on knit rows and from left to right on purl rows. Twist the yarns in back of the work when changing colors and don't carry the yarn more than 3 stitches without twisting.

RIGHT SLIPPER LEG

Using the green yarn and straight needles, cast on 32(34,36) sts.

Rib in k1, p1 for 12 rows.

Work 2 rows stockinette stitch.

Begin Santa graph at the hat.

Work a total of 5" (12.7 cm), including the ribbed cuff.

If your Santa is not finished in 5" (12.7 cm), finish him as you knit the gusset.

HEEL TAB

Put the center front half of the stitches on a holder.

Attach yarn to back half and work 12 rows to form the heel tab.

Bind off.

GUSSET

Using dp needles and with right side facing, pick up and knit 12 sts along right side of heel tab.

Place a marker.

Knit across front instep on design if necessary.

Place a marker.

Pick up 12 sts along left side of heel tab.

Purl back, slipping markers.

On next and all following knit rows, dec as follows:

Knit to within 2 sts of marker.

K2 tog.

Sip marker.

Work to next marker.

Slip marker.

K2 tog.

Knit to end.

Purl back.

Repeat until 20(20,22) sts remain.

Remove markers.

Simultaneously, when the graph design is complete, work 2 rows and center cable on foot.

Begin toe when foot measures 6(6½,7)" (15.2,16.5,17.8 cm) from center of heel tab.

TOE

Dec 1 st each end every knit row until 8 sts remain.

Bind off.

LEFT SLIPPER

Work as for right, inserting cable pattern on leg and Santa on foot.

For cable pattern, work on center 10 sts:

Rows 1, 3, 5 (right side rows): P2, k6, p2.

Rows 2, 4, 6 (wrong side rows): K2, p6, k2.

Row 7: K2, slip 3 sts to back on cable needle, k3, k3 from cable needle, p2.

Work toe as for right slipper.

Bind off.

FINISHING

Using tapestry needle and whip stitch, attach socks to moccasin soles.

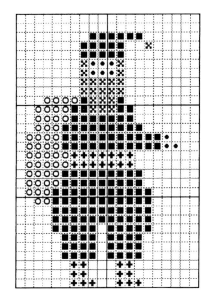

KEY TO CHART

■ = Red

● = Pink

✖ = White

+ = Black

O = Tan

DESIGN: GAY SYMMES
SIZES: CHILDREN'S 2, 4, AND 6

ORDIC SANTA PULLOVER

As a knitting designer and grandmother, Gay Symmes finds many occasions to create custom sweaters for children.

Her love of Christmas inspired this cozy pullover, with its colorful arrangement of Santas,

Christmas trees, hearts, and snowflakes on the front and back.

MATERIALS & TOOLS

- approximately 11 oz. (300 g) white worsted-weight yarn
- 2 oz. (57 g) each of green and red worsted-weight yarn
- scraps of black and pink yarn
- knitting needles: 1 pair #3, 1 pair #5, 1 set #3 dp
- stitch holders
- bobbins
- tapestry needle

INSTRUCTIONS

Instructions are for sizes 2(4,6) and gauge is 5½ sts = 1" (2.5 cm). When changing colors, twist the yarns. Keep the design centered; it's perfectly acceptable to add or subtract a stitch to do so. Do not carry yarn across more than 5 sts behind work.

FRONT

With green yarn and smaller needles, cast on 64(68,72) sts.

Rib in k1, p1 for 1½" (3.8 cm).

Changing to larger needles and white yarn, begin chart at lower right corner. For size 2, omit first and last hearts on chart.

After working the hearts, change background color to green for Santas.

Return to white for trees and top.

When the piece measures 8(9,10)" (20.3,22.9,25.4 cm), dec for armhole by binding off 3 sts at beginning next 2 rows.

Dec 1 st each end next 2 knit rows.

Work even until armhole measures 3½(4,4½)" (8.9,10.2,11.4 cm).

Work 18(20,22) sts.

Bind off next 21 sts for front neck.

With 2 balls of yarn, work sides separately.

Dec 1 st at neck edge on knit row 2 times to give 16(18,20) sts each side.

Work even until armholes measure 5(5½,6)" (12.7,14,15.2 cm) from original armhole dec.

Bind off.

BACK

Work same as front using same graph or work all-over snowflake pattern.

Do not divide for neck.

Work even until armholes measure same as front.

Bind off 16(18,20) sts at beginning next 2 rows.

Place remaining sts on holder for neck.

SLEEVES

Using smaller needles and green yarn, cast on 40 sts.

Rib in k1, p1 for 1½" (3.8 cm), inc 5 sts in last row.

Change to white and do snowflake design every 4 rows.

Simultaneously, inc 1 st each end every 1" (2.5 cm) until you have 53(57,61) sts.

Work even until piece measures 11(12,13)" (27.9,30.5,33 cm).

Bind off 3 sts at beginning next 2 rows.

Bind off 1 st each knit row each end until 31 sts remain.

Bind off 3 sts at beginning next 4 rows.

Bind off remaining sts.

NECK

Sew shoulder seam.

With white yarn, right side facing, and dp needles, pick up 67 to 70 sts around neck, including sts from holder.

Rib in k1, p1 for 4 rounds.

Change to green.

Knit 1 round.

Return to rib pattern for 1 round.

Bind off loosely in pattern.

FINISHING

Weave in all loose ends.

Insert sleeves and sew side seams.

Block as needed.

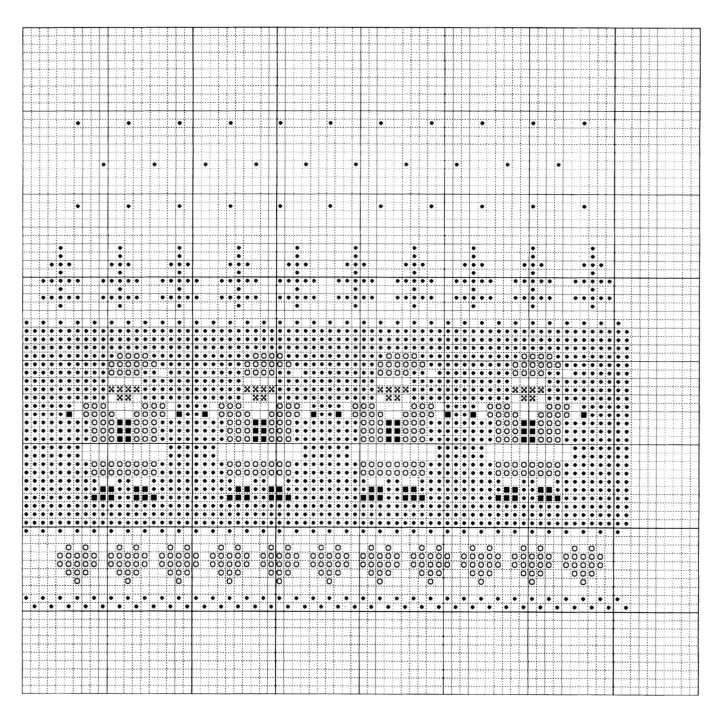

KEY TO CHART

- ● = Green
- ■ = Black
- ✖ = Pink
- ○ = Red
- ☐ = White

DESIGN: PAT SCHEIBLE
SIZE: 14" x 4" (35.6 x 10.2 CM)

SANTA AND SLEIGH CHAPEAU

Artist Pat Scheible is unequaled in her talent for recycling the ordinary into something truly special. Here a simple felt hat becomes a conversation piece with the addition of some inexpensive figurines and plenty of imagination.

MATERIALS & TOOLS

- burgundy felt hat with wide brim and ribbon trim
- Santa, sleigh, and reindeer figurines
- acrylic paints
- artist's brush
- gold doilies
- glue gun
- fine red cord
- sprig of artificial fruit

INSTRUCTIONS

1 ▪ Most inexpensive figurines are poorly painted. Take some time to make the colors more realistic and to add some detailed touches. For example, accenting the trim on Santa's sleigh with gold paint gives him a more majestic vehicle for his nighttime journey.

2 ▪ Cut pieces from gold doilies to use as decorative saddles and spot-glue the pieces onto the reindeer.

3 ▪ Glue Santa into his sleigh, together with a small piece of artificial evergreen if desired, and position the sleigh on the brim of the hat. Place the reindeer where desired and secure them with hot glue.

4 ▪ Starting at the front reindeer and working back to the sleigh, thread two lengths of fine red cord through the doily pieces. These become the reins.

5 ▪ Add a final flourish by gluing a sprig of artificial fruit onto the ribbon trim.

 ANTA'S ARRIVAL

As the mercury drops in time for the holiday season, any child will welcome the chance to wear this cheery pullover designed by Gay Symmes. The front features Santa in his sleigh, and four reindeer prance across a starry sky on the back.

MATERIALS & TOOLS

- 7(11,11) oz. (200,300,300 g) navy blue worsted-weight yarn
- 1 skein each of white and red worsted-weight yarn
- short lengths of green, tan, and gray yarn
- knitting needles: 1 pair #3, 1 pair #5, 1 set #3 dp
- stitch holders
- bobbins
- tapestry needle

DESIGN: GAY SYMMES
SIZES: CHILDREN'S 2, 4, AND 6

INSTRUCTIONS

Instructions are for sizes 2(4,6) and gauge is 5½ sts = 1" (2.5 cm). When changing colors, twist the yarns. Keep the design centered; it's perfectly acceptable to add or subtract a stitch to do so. Do not carry yarn across more than 5 sts behind work. Work graph from right side on knit rows and from left side on purl rows.

FRONT

With red yarn and smaller needles, cast on 63(67,71) sts.

Rib in k1, p1 for 1 row.

Change to navy and knit across all stitches.

Return to k1, p1 ribbing and continue for total of 1½" (3.8 cm). End with a wrong side row.

Change to larger needles and stockinette stitch with red for 9 rows.

Change to white for 9 rows.

Begin graph on a knit row.

When total piece measures 8(9,10)" (20.3,22.9,25.4 cm), bind off 3 sts at beginning next 2 rows.

Dec 1 st each end next 2 knit rows.

Work even until armhole measures 3½(4,4½)" (8.9,10.2,11.4 cm).

Work 18(20,22) sts.

Bind off 21 sts for front neck.

With two balls of yarn, work sides separately.

Dec 1 st at neck edge on next 2 knit rows to give 16(18,20) sts on each shoulder.

Work even until armholes measure 5(5½,6)" (12.7,14,15.2 cm).

Bind off.

BACK

Using back graph, work same as front but do not divide for neck.

Work even until armholes measure same as front.

Bind off 16(18,20) sts next 2 rows for shoulders.

Put center sts on holder for back of neck.

SLEEVES

Using smaller needles and red yarn, cast on 40 sts.

Work 1 row ribbing.

Change to navy and knit across row.

Return to ribbing pattern for total of 1½" (3.8 cm).

Increase 5 sts in last row.

Change to larger needles and stockinette stitch.

Increase 1 st each end of knit row each 1" (2.5 cm) until you have 53(57,61) sts.

Work even to 11(12,13)" (27.9,30.5,33 cm).

Bind off 3 sts at beginning next 2 rows.

Bind off 1 st each end every knit row until you have 31 sts.

Bind off 3 sts at beginning next 4 rows.

Bind off remaining sts.

NECK

Sew shoulder seams.

With navy yarn, right side facing, and set of #3 dp needles, pick up 67 to 70 sts, including ones from holder.

Rib k1, p1 for 4 rounds.

Change to red and knit 1 row all the way around.

Return to rib pattern for 1 row.

Bind off loosely in pattern.

FINISHING

With white yarn, use duplicate stitch to sprinkle snowflakes in sky around Santa's sled and around reindeer.

Insert sleeves and sew underarm seams.

Weave in all loose ends.

Block as needed.

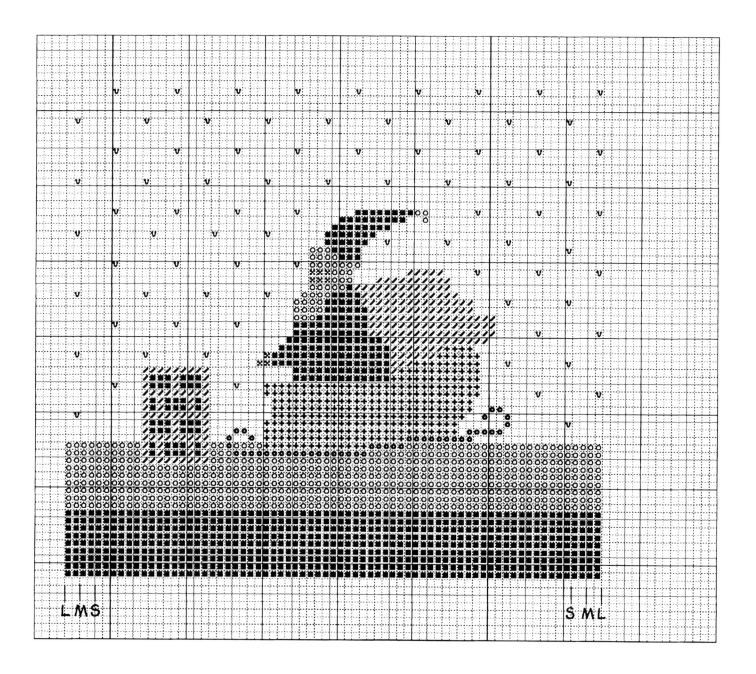

KEY TO BOTH CHARTS

■ = Red			⊙ = Gray	
⊙ = White			+ = Green	
╱ = Tan			∩ = White (duplicate stitch)	
▨ = Pink			● = Blue	

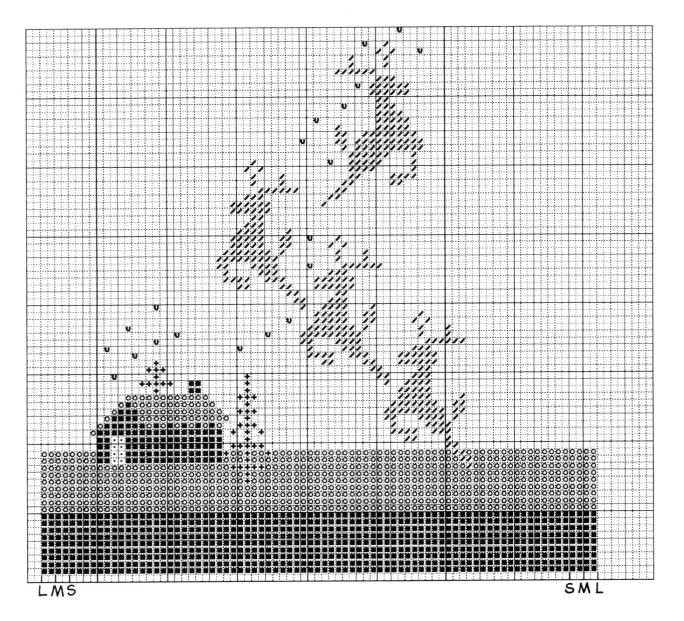

LMS

SML

ELFIN SANTA

Small in size but large in spirit, this whimsical Santa designed by Terry Taylor is certain to bring good cheer to all your holiday festivities. He has lots of personality tucked into his compact body, yet his features are simple enough for a beginner to carve.

DESIGN: TERRY TAYLOR
SIZE: 4" (10.2 CM) TALL

MATERIALS & TOOLS

- 1¾" x 1¾" x 4¼" (4.4 x 4.4 x 10.8 cm) block of basswood
- transfer pen or soft pencil
- carving knife or pocketknife
- small veining chisel (optional)
- sandpaper
- acrylic paints
- gold enamel paint
- acrylic varnish or paste wax
- assorted small paintbrushes
- toothpick
- jigsaw or motorized "mini-tool"

INSTRUCTIONS

1 ▪ Sketch an outline of your Santa onto the block of wood or enlarge and transfer the outline in *figure 1*.

2 ▪ Begin carving by roughly defining the boot area and cutting away the area between the boots. Then rough out the overall shape of the face, beard, and arms, rounding the edges and turning the block frequently.

3 ▪ Carve the top the block into a point. Near the top of the point, incise a line around and begin to shape the fur ball.

4 ▪ Use the tip of your knife to incise the sketched lines of the beard, face, and arms. Then begin to remove small amounts of wood from the areas outside the lines. The arms, beard, and facial areas are in light relief, so don't carve too deeply.

5 ▪ Working carefully, define the nose, cheeks, and eyebrows with your knife. Use sandpaper as you go along to help refine the facial features.

6 ▪ Add texture to the beard and fur ball by incising them with your knife and making small valley cuts. For this purpose a small veining chisel is helpful.

7 ▪ When you have finished carving and sanding, apply a base coat of acrylic paint to the entire surface and allow it to dry.

8 ▪ As you apply the final colors, paint each area and allow it to dry before painting the next. Start by applying skin tone to the facial area. While the paint is still wet, mix in a bit of red and highlight the cheeks. Follow with the beard, eyebrows, and fur ball. Then paint the suit, mittens, and boots.

9 ▪ Use a brush with a small handle end to make the eyes. Dip the end of the handle in blue paint and apply a dot of paint where each eye belongs. Allow the paint to dry. Then, using a toothpick, make tiny black and white highlights in each eye dot.

10 ▪ Use the handle end of a small brush to cover the robe area with gold enamel polka dots.

11 ▪ When the paint is dry, protect the surface with a coat of acrylic varnish or paste wax.

CARVING & SCULPTING

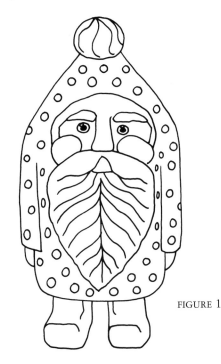

FIGURE 1

ᚠATHER CHRISTMAS

When drawing or sculpting a face, we often unconsciously model the features after those of someone we know.

Everyone in Diane Kuebitz's family agrees that if the beard were removed from this Santa figure,

he would look just like her father!

DESIGN: Diane Kuebitz
SIZE: 7" (17.8 cm) TALL

MATERIALS & TOOLS

- aluminum foil
- toothpicks
- polymer clay: less than one package each of red, white, black, gold, and flesh
- rolling pin or pasta machine (do not use for food afterward)
- sculpting tools, sharp and blunt
- sharp knife
- safety pin
- blue, white, black acrylic paints
- pink chalk
- fine-tipped paintbrush
- baking sheet

INSTRUCTIONS

1 ▪ Make an armature for your figure by shaping aluminum foil into a cone about 6" (15.2 cm) tall with a 2" (5.1 cm) base. Add some extra foil around the middle for a fat tummy. Flatten a 2" (5.1-cm) ball of red clay into a sheet ⅛" (3 mm) thick and set the aluminum cone in the center. Press the clay up around the sides of the cone.

2 ▪ Insert a toothpick into the top of the cone to support the head. Roll a ¾" (1.9-cm) ball of white clay into an egg shape and press the small end onto the toothpick. Wrap a small strip of white clay around the bottom for a neck and indent the face side of the egg with your thumb.

3 ▪ Form a 1" (2.5-cm) ball of black clay into a boot, marking a sole line around the bottom with a sharp sculpting tool. Shape a ⅜" (1-cm) ball into the front section of a second boot. Press both boots onto the foil armature. Then bake the assembly for 45 minutes at the temperature recommended by the clay manufacturer.

4 ▪ Press a ¾" (1.9-cm) ball of flesh-colored clay into the face indentation on the head. Flatten another ¾" ball into a sheet; use this to cover the neck and the top and back of the head. Smooth the seams and shape a chin.

5 ▪ With a sharp tool, draw a mouth. Shape two ⅜" (1-cm) balls of clay into triangles for lips. Use a blunt tool to indent the middle of the upper lip and place both over the mouth line, blending the seams.

6 ▪ To make cheeks, roll two ½" (1.3-cm) balls of skin-colored clay into comma shapes and flatten them slightly. Press them onto the face and smooth the seams gently. Blend the outer seams of the cheeks into the head and indent the eye sockets.

7 ▪ Roll a ½" (1.3-cm) ball of flesh-colored clay into a short cone and position it for the nose.

8 ▪ Make two ⅛" (3-mm) balls of white clay and bake them for 15 minutes. When they're cool, press these into the eye sockets. Use the pointed end of a toothpick to make tear ducts. Roll four tiny snakelike pieces of skin-colored clay and press these above and below the eyes for eyelids.

9 ▪ For the robe, flatten a 2" (5.1-cm) ball of red clay into a large sheet. Cut two pieces for the front and one for the back (*fig. 1*). Join the front pieces to the back by pinching the seams gently.

10 ▪ Roll a ⅜"-diameter (1-cm) rope of white clay and attach it to the edges of the robe. Texture the white with the end of a safety pin to make it look like fur. Wrap the robe around the armature and gently press it closed over the figure.

11 ▪ To make sleeves, roll a cylinder of red clay ³⁄₁₆" x 1½" (.5 x 3.8 cm). Insert the end of a pencil about ¾" (1.9 cm) into one end. Hold the sleeve with one hand and roll the pencil back and forth with the other. Bend the sleeve at the elbow and press it onto the shoulder of the figure. Repeat with the second sleeve and add fur trim to both.

12. Roll two ½" (1.3-cm) balls of flesh-colored clay and shape the hands. Use the sharp tool to make wrinkles in the knuckles and fingernail indentations. Pinch them gently into the sleeves.

13. Shape a 1" (2.5-cm) ball of red clay into a triangle. Drape this behind the head for a hood. Add white fur around the edge.

14. Flatten some white clay into a sheet 5" x 5" (12.7 x 12.7 cm). Cut four or five thin strands and attach them gently to the figure's bald head. Twist the strands for a curled effect. Continue until the entire head is covered; then use smaller pieces for the eyebrows, mustache, and beard.

15. Make a small, bowl-shaped cap of red clay to cover the top of Santa's head. Trim it with white fur and gently press it in place.

16. Flatten a ¾"-diameter (1.9-cm) log of black clay and wrap it around the waist for a belt. Use the gold clay to shape a buckle.

17. Place the figure on the baking sheet and bake for one hour at the temperature recommended by the clay manufacturer.

18. When the figure is cool, paint the eyes with acrylic paints and add a blush to the cheeks with pink chalk. If desired, hot-glue a small stick in one hand.

FRONT
CUT 2

BACK
CUT 1

FIGURE 1

DANCING SANTA

Santa isn't often noted for his graceful moves, but in this lively figure, artist Alice Lawson has endowed him with an elegant sweep of the cape and plenty of implied motion. To emphasize the beauty of the carving, don't sand away all the knife marks from the surface of the wood.

DESIGN: ALICE M. LAWSON
SIZE: 9¼" (23.5 CM) TALL

MATERIALS & TOOLS

- block of basswood 6½" x 9½" x 3½" (16.5 x 24.1 x 8.9 cm)
- carving knife
- band saw
- large #3 palm gouge
- large palm V tool
- set of small palm gouges
- carving glove (recommended)
- paints: red, ivory, black, blue, skin tone
- artist's brushes
- brown shoe polish paste
- old toothbrush

INSTRUCTIONS

1 ▪ After tracing the pattern (*fig. 1*) onto your wood, cut out the Santa using a knife or band saw. Mark the center line, front and back.

2 ▪ Round the edges and begin shaping the figure with the knife or wide #3 gouge. Using *figure 1* as a guide, remove significant amounts of wood to form the arms, hands, robe, and hood.

3 ▪ Refine the shape and add details next. With the large V tool, carve the outline for the fur, beard, face, hood, and hands. Deep cuts should separate the sleeves from the coat. To carve the fur, first remove wood from the skirt, robe, face, and back of the hood. Carve away part of the robe to make the beard, noting that the beard overlaps the fur and front of the robe. Remove part of the skirt to reveal the shoe. Carve the back of the figure so that the robe is flowing and the hood distinct.

4 ▪ Santa's oval-shaped face should rest back in the hood, with the nose forming the most prominent point and the eyes the deepest. The eyes are located nearly halfway down the face (*fig. 2*). With the large V tool, cut across the face to form the bridge of the nose and eye sockets. Make the cut fairly deep.

5 ▪ Define the nose with the V tool, cutting down both sides and under the nose. Make the cuts deeper at the corners of the eyes.

6 ▪ Outline the cheeks with the V tool, making them fat and puffy. Then carve down the beard under the nose and cheeks. Periodically view your Santa from the side to make sure you're getting the appropriate contours.

7 ▪ Now carve the hair with a small V tool or U gouge. Remember to shape the mustache, which lies on top of the beard.

8 ▪ Shape the eyes with the small V tool. Make four cuts to form the shape of an eye (*fig. 3*). Then, starting in the corners, make small deep cuts with the tip of your knife. Slice back to the corners and remove the V-shaped chip on each side of the eye.

9 ▪ Shape the forehead and hair. With a small V tool, make lines for the eyebrows.

10 ▪ After cleaning up any ragged areas, wash your Santa with soap and water, scrubbing it with a toothbrush. This removes oil, dirt, and small bits of excess wood.

11 ▪ Saving the eyes until last, paint your figure. Paint the complete eye with ivory paint and let it dry. Then add a circle of blue in the center. After it has dried, add a circle of black. To give the eyes a twinkle, place a small dot of ivory paint on the side of each eye.

12 ▪ Using the toothbrush, totally cover your Santa with a thin coating of shoe polish. Immediately wipe off the excess with a soft cloth. Use a toothpick for reaching deep corners and cuts.

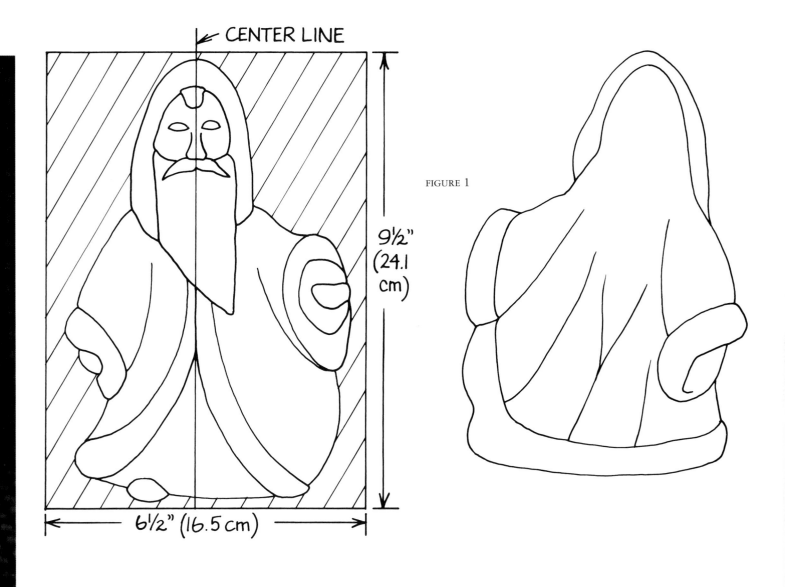

CENTER LINE

9½"
(24.1
cm)

6½" (16.5 cm)

FIGURE 1

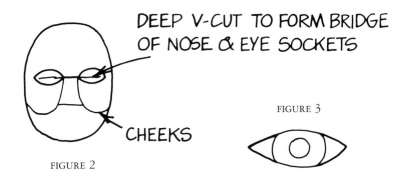

DEEP V-CUT TO FORM BRIDGE
OF NOSE & EYE SOCKETS

CHEEKS

FIGURE 2

FIGURE 3

DESIGN: DAVID VANCE
SIZE: 19" (48.3 CM) TALL WHEN STANDING

JOINTED WOODEN SANTA

David Vance created this articulated folk art Santa to be displayed as a door decoration. He used pieces of poplar siding that had been removed from a small country church near his home, but the design can be adapted to any size wood for other decorative applications.

MATERIALS & TOOLS

- any type of wood board 1" x 5" x 12" (2.5 x 12.7 x 30.5 cm)
- wood board 1" x 4" x 12" (2.5 x 10.2 x 30.5 cm)
- wood board 1" x 1½" x 24" (2.5 x 3.8 x 61 cm)
- transfer pen or soft pencil
- electric drill with ⅛" (3-mm) and ³⁄₁₆" (5-mm) bits
- jigsaw or band saw
- motorized "mini-tool" with sanding wheels and carving and sanding bits (or wood rasp, wood file, and carving knife)
- acrylic paints
- small paintbrushes
- sandpaper
- walnut stain
- satin acrylic sealer
- nails or screws
- short piece of ⅛" (3-mm) dowel
- carpenter's wood glue

INSTRUCTIONS

1 ▪ Draw the main pattern pieces (*fig. 1*) onto the wood; use the 4" (10.2-cm) board for the arms and the 1½" (3.8-cm) board for the legs and feet.

2 ▪ Before cutting the notches on the body and legs, drill the holes through the edges, as indicated in *figure 1*. Then cut the pieces with a jigsaw or band saw.

3 ▪ Using the sanding attachments on a motorized tool, or a rasp and file, round the edges of the pieces and refine the shapes.

4 ▪ Sketch the outlines of a face and beard (or transfer the design in *figure 1*) onto the top portion of the main body piece. Using the motorized tool or carving knife, lightly carve the facial features. Keep the carving fairly simple—using broad strokes to suggest the desired shapes—and in low relief to maintain the folk art appearance.

5 ▪ If desired, use the "mini-tool" or knife to cut some additional strokes in the body to distinguish the fur trim of the coat and the belt.

6 ▪ When you're satisfied with the carving, apply a base coat of white acrylic paint to all the pieces. Then, using the colors of your choice, paint the face, body, and limbs.

7 ▪ To give your Santa the look of an antique piece, lightly sand the painted surface to reveal small areas of the base coat and underlying wood. Then wipe walnut stain over the entire surface. Before it dries, wipe away most of the stain, leaving only small amounts in the crevices. Allow the stain to dry; then apply a coat of clear satin acrylic sealer.

8 ▪ Attach the arms to the body and the feet to the legs with short nails or screws. To assemble the articulated joints, apply wood glue inside all of the ⅛" (3-mm) holes and insert 1½" (3.8-cm) lengths of the dowel through the appropriate pieces. The ³⁄₁₆" (5-mm) holes in the outward-facing notches aren't glued, which allows the legs to move freely.

FIGURE 1

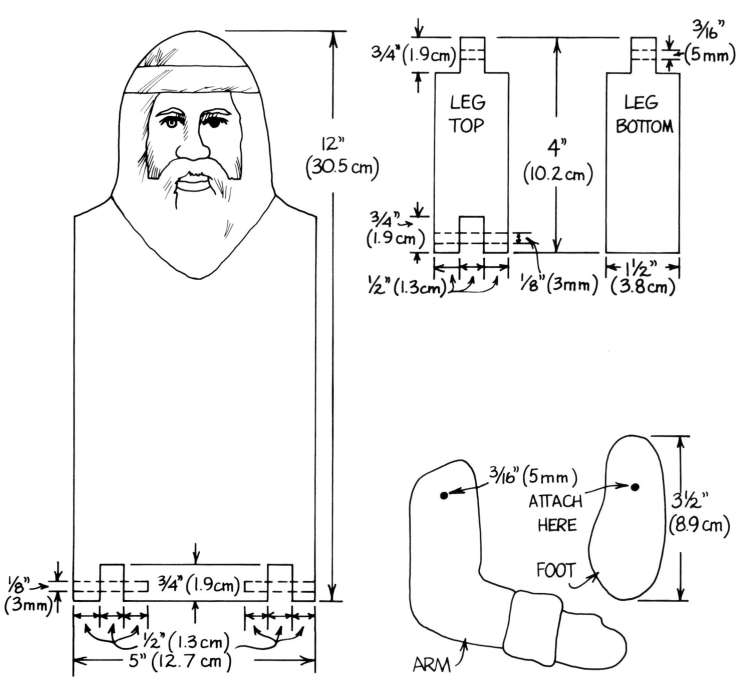

12"
(30.5 cm)

3/4"(1.9 cm)

LEG
TOP

3/4"
(1.9 cm)

1/2"(1.3 cm)

4"
(10.2 cm)

1/8"(3mm)

3/16"
(5mm)

LEG
BOTTOM

1½"
(3.8 cm)

1/8"
(3mm)

3/4"(1.9cm)

1/2"(1.3cm)

5"(12.7 cm)

3/16"(5mm)
ATTACH
HERE

FOOT

3½"
(8.9 cm)

ARM

GOLDEN MYSTIC SANTA

Terry Taylor has endowed this carved wooden figure with a good measure of fantasy, from the tip of his mile-high turban to the end of his full-length beard. His sunny yellow robes—a departure from the traditional red—are covered in bright golden stars.

DESIGN: Terry Taylor
SIZE: 11½" (29.2 CM) TALL

MATERIALS & TOOLS

- block of basswood or other soft wood 1" x 1¼" x 12" (2.5 x 3.2 x 30.5 cm)
- 2 pieces of basswood 1" x 1¼" x 3½" (2.5 x 3.2 x 8.9 cm)
- pencil or transfer pen and paper
- jigsaw or motorized "mini-tool"
- drill with ¼" (6-mm) bit
- 2 dowels ¼" dia. x 1" (0.6 x 2.5 cm)
- carving knife or pocketknife
- small veining chisel
- sandpaper
- acrylic paints
- small paintbrushes
- toothpicks
- clear acrylic finish
- carpenter's wood glue

INSTRUCTIONS

1 ▪ Enlarge *figure 1* and transfer the outline and features—or sketch your own design—onto the larger block of wood. Then rough out the boots and point of the hat with the saw or "mini-tool."

2 ▪ To make the arms, first mark their positions on the sides of the block; then drill a hole ½" (1.3 cm) deep on each side. Sketch the general shape of the arms on the small blocks of wood. On each inside edge (the side that will face the body), drill a hole about ½" deep.

3 ▪ Begin to rough out the general shape of the figure by rounding off the sharp edges of the main block. Using the point of your knife, incise lines for the trim, beard, face, hair, and hat. To make the twist in the peaked hat, make a long diagonal mark that twists around the block of wood. Then cut toward the incised lines, making a small valley along each one to define important features.

4 ▪ Continue to shape the figure by rounding the edges. Because this is more a fantasy figure than a realistic one, don't be constrained in your carving. In the facial area, concentrate on defining the eyebrows, nose, and cheeks. Use the small veining chisel to give depth to the beard and hair areas. If you don't have a small chisel, you can achieve a similar effect with the point of your knife by making deep incised lines followed by small valley cuts.

5 ▪ Round out the arm forms, leaving the inner side relatively flat to fit against the body, and shape mittens for hands.

6 ▪ To remove knife marks and smooth the surface, sand the body and arms as desired.

7 ▪ Insert the dowels into the body and glue them in place with wood glue. Leave the arms unattached for now.

8 ▪ Prepare the figure for painting by applying a base coat of acrylic paint. Once this is dry, lightly sand it.

9 ▪ When painting your Santa, use one color at a time and allow it to dry before moving on to the next area. Begin with the body, hat, and arms. Yellow tends not to cover well, so you may need several coats. Paint the face next, mixing a bit of darker pink or red into the skin tone to accent the cheek and lip areas. Follow with the beard, hair, and eyebrows. Then paint the ivory trim, green mittens, and black boots.

10 ▪ To make the eyes, dip the end of the brush handle into some white paint and make two small dots where the eyes should be. After these have dried, add small dots of brown paint applied with the wider end of a toothpick. Then use the finer tip of the toothpick to apply a tiny white highlight on each eye.

11 ▪ To make the decorative star pattern on Santa's coat, dip the end of the brush handle in gold paint and apply a dot of paint to the coat; then use the handle as you would a pencil to draw the star points out from the center. It's best to practice this technique on scraps first before committing yourself. Cover the coat, hat, and sleeves as desired.

12 ▪ Once all the paint is dry, glue the arms to the body. Then apply one or more coats of acrylic finish.

FIGURE 1

OLYMER CLAY SAINT NICHOLAS

Maureen Carlson is renowned for her lifelike representations of people, and one of her favorite subjects is Santa. This figure is easier to create than you might think because the hands and face are made using readily available push molds.

DESIGN: MAUREEN CARLSON
SIZE: 8" (20.3 CM) TALL

MATERIALS & TOOLS

- polymer clay: 5 packages of champagne; 1 each of red, bronze, flesh, midnight blue, fir green, and white; about ½ package of scrap clay (any color)
- polymer clay kneading medium
- aluminum foil
- 8" (20.3 cm) coat hanger wire
- 2 baking sheets
- paintbrushes
- baby powder or cornstarch
- What A Character push molds #10 and #12
- 2 blue seed beads
- pink chalk or matte blush
- parchment paper
- brown acrylic paint
- oven
- rolling pin
- knife
- darning needle or toothpick
- textured cloth
- ruler

INSTRUCTIONS

1 ▪ Condition all of the clay, using a kneading medium if desired.

2 ▪ To make an armature, crumple the aluminum foil into a pudgy cone. Make a flat base for the cone using a sheet of scrap polymer clay about ⅛" (3 mm) thick. Apply more of the scrap clay to the shoulder and chest area of the foil. To strengthen the neck, bend the wire in half and twist the top into a loop. Insert this into the top of the armature. Roll a ball of clay 1¼" (3.2 cm) in diameter and press this onto the back of the wire loop to form the back of the head. Smooth the clay into the shoulders (*fig. 1*).

3 ▪ Set the armature on a baking sheet and place it in a preheated oven set to the temperature recommended by the clay manufacturer. Bake for 30 minutes.

4 ▪ To make the head, roll a 1¼"-diameter (3.2-cm) ball of flesh-colored clay. Then form the ball into a pointed cone shape. Brush the face mold lightly with powder. Using your thumb, firmly push the point of the cone into the nose of the mold. Remove the molded head and place it over the front of the armature, smoothing the edges of the face into the neck and sides of the head.

5 ▪ Use a darning needle or toothpick to add detail to the nostrils and mouth and to create wrinkles around the eyes. With the same tool, insert seed beads into the eyes so that the center hole forms the pupil. Insert the beads slightly deeper than the eyelids and pull the forehead slightly toward the eyes to cause the lids to cover the top edges of the beads.

6 ▪ Brush powdered chalk or blush onto the cheeks and nose.

7 ▪ Flatten the champagne clay into a sheet slightly thinner than ⅛" (3 mm) and cut the pieces shown in *figure 2*. Cut two pieces, the front robe and back portion of the outer robe, following the solid lines; then cut the two side/front pieces of the outer robe following the dotted lines. Press all four pieces with a lint-free fabric to add texture.

8 ▪ Position the front robe piece onto the armature, pressing firmly at the neck edge and gently draping it into soft folds. Add a strip of bronze clay for a belt and buckle. Then assemble the three pieces of the outside robe by slightly overlapping the edges. Set this aside to make the trim.

9 ▪ To make the patchwork trim, first mix some lighter tones by combining champagne clay with the other colors. Add some bronze to the red to create a darker tone. Roll the rusty red clay into a rope and flatten it into a long strip about ⅜" (1.6 cm) wide and 1/16" (1.6 mm) thick. Then flatten small strips of the other colors. Cut small patches of these and press them onto the long strip to form patchwork. Add texture by pressing the surface with fabric; then use the needle to add stitch lines. Attach the trim around the edges of the robe.

10 ▪ Position the robe around the shoulders of the figure, pressing in soft gathers at the back of the neck. Be sure that the bottom edge is snug enough to conceal the foil armature.

11 ▪ To make the sleeves, roll two 1¼" (3.2-cm) balls and form each into a 2½"-long (6.4-cm) rope. Use a sturdy brush handle or wooden dowel to hollow each sleeve to the elbow. Add texture, patchwork trim, and wrinkle lines at the elbows.

12 ▪ Begin the hands by rolling two ropes of flesh-colored clay slightly narrower than the width of the mold. Form one end of each rope into a mitten shape and press it into the mold, taking care not to overflow the mold. Remove the hand from the mold and shape the palm and wrist. Then insert the hand into the sleeve, pinching the sleeve securely around the wrist.

13 ▪ Mix the white clay with a small amount of champagne to give it a variegated look for the beard and hair. After flattening it into a sheet ⅛" (3 mm) thick, cut several thin strands. Twist them and add a few at a time to make the beard.

14 ▪ Apply short textured pieces for the eyebrows, mustache, and hair, keeping them fairly close to the body to guard against breakage later.

15 ▪ For a hat, roll a 1½" (3.8-cm) ball of champagne clay into a 4"-tall (10.2-cm) cone with a 1¼"-diameter (3.2-cm) base. Use a dowel or brush handle to hollow out the cone until it will fit over the head. Add patchwork trim and a rusty red tassel for embellishments.

16 ▪ To guard against uneven oven heat, bake the completed figure on a doubled baking sheet. Preheat the oven to the recommended temperature and bake for 30 to 60 minutes. Cool the figure in the oven before removing it.

17 ▪ After cooling, add details to the eyes by stroking a light brown wash into the surrounding wrinkles. Add eyeliner to define the eyes. To make Santa's list, roll a small piece of parchment and place it in one hand.

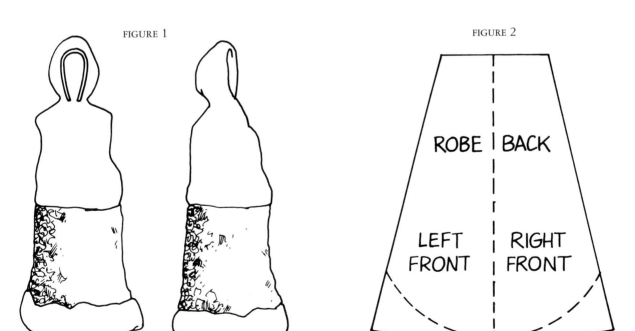

FIGURE 1

FIGURE 2

ROBE | BACK

LEFT FRONT | RIGHT FRONT

PLACE MATS WITH NAPKINS AND RINGS

DESIGN: MARY PARKER
SIZE: PLACE MAT, 18" x 13" (45.7 x 33 CM);
NAPKIN, 15" (38.1 CM) SQUARE;
RING, 2" x 7" (5.1 x 17.8 CM)

Hand-sewn place mats with matching napkins and rings are certain to fit any size table perfectly.

Mary Parker has designed these with Santa and his reindeer-drawn sleigh in full flight,

arcing across the night sky.

MATERIALS & TOOLS
(for a set of four)

- 2⅝ yds. (2.4 m) red fabric 45" (114.3 cm) wide
- ¾ yd. (68.6 cm) fusible fleece
- dark iron-on transfer pen
- tracing paper
- white topstitching thread
- machine needle with large eye for topstitching thread
- sewing thread
- sewing machine
- hook-and-loop tape
- roll of fusible web tape
- hand-sewing needle with large eye

INSTRUCTIONS

1 ▪ From the red fabric cut four place mats 17" x 22" (43.2 x 55.9 cm), four place mat backings 13" x 18" (33 x 45.7 cm), four napkin squares 16" x 16" (40.6 x 40.6 cm), and four napkin rings 4" x 8" (10.2 x 20.3 cm) as shown in *figure 1*.

2 ▪ Cut four rectangles 18" x 13" (45.7 x 33 cm) and four strips 2" x 7" (5.1 x 17.8 cm) from the fusible fleece (*fig. 2*).

3 ▪ To angle the corners of the place mats, mark 2" (5.1 cm) back from each corner on the long edge and 1½" (3.8 cm) back from each corner on the short edge. Draw a line between the marks and cut. Repeat with each of the large rectangles of fusible fleece.

4 ▪ Using a zigzag stitch, sew around all the edges of the four larger place mat pieces to prevent raveling and to make an attractive finished edge (which will be visible on the underside). Then zigzag around the edges of the napkin rings.

5 ▪ To create the fringed edges on the napkins, stitch ½" (1.3 cm) from the edge, pivoting at each corner. Pull a few threads to start the process; then wash the napkins once or twice to get the full amount of fringe. Secure them from further raveling by stitching a narrow, dense zigzag stitch over your first line of sewing. This completes the napkins.

6 ▪ Center one small strip of fleece on the wrong side of each napkin ring and fuse into place. Set these aside.

7 ▪ Center one of the rectangles of fusible fleece on the wrong side of each of the larger place mat pieces and fuse.

8 ▪ Using an iron-on transfer pen, transfer the pattern outline in *figure 3* to the fleece side of each place mat.

9 ▪ Adjust the bobbin tension in your machine to accommodate the heavier topstitching thread. Wind a bobbin or two with topstitching thread and place regular white sewing thread in the needle.

10 ▪ Before you begin sewing, pull out at least 4" (10.2 cm) of needle and bobbin threads to use later to tie off the ends. Start each pair of reindeer at the point indicated in *figure 3* and continue sewing until you return to your starting point. Leave a tail at least 4" long on both bobbin and sewing threads before cutting them. Remove the place mat from the machine, thread the bobbin thread through a hand-sewing needle, and pull it through to the fusible fleece side. After tying off both sets of threads, continue until all four pairs of reindeer are complete.

HOLIDAY DINING

11 . To sew the sleigh, follow the outside edge and tie off the threads as before. Then sew the series of blocks that define the sled runners, again tying off the threads.

12 . When you've completed all the stitching, set each place mat right side down on an ironing board and place a backing piece of fabric on the fusible fleece, trimming the corners to match the place mat. Fuse the backing in place; then fold and press the overextending portions of the place mat back onto the backing. When these have been pressed satisfactorily, anchor them in place by inserting thin strips of the fusible web between the fabrics.

13 . Now fold and press the overextending portions of the napkin rings onto the wrong sides. Secure the edges as necessary with fusible web tape.

14 . Load white sewing thread into your bobbin (and adjust the tension) and thread the topstitching thread through the needle. With the place mat right side up, topstitch about ½" (1.3 cm) around the edges. Repeat with the other three place mats; then topstitch along the long edges of each napkin ring.

15 . Secure the tucked-in short edges of the napkin rings by topstitching those ends with red matching thread. Then attach the hook-and-loop fasteners to the ends of each ring.

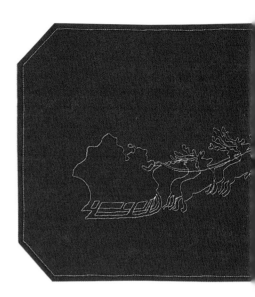

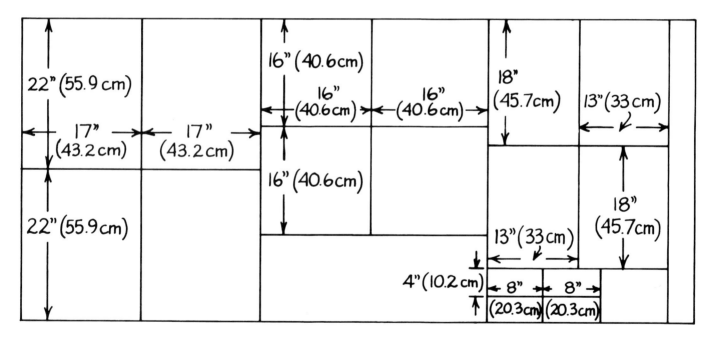

FIGURE 1

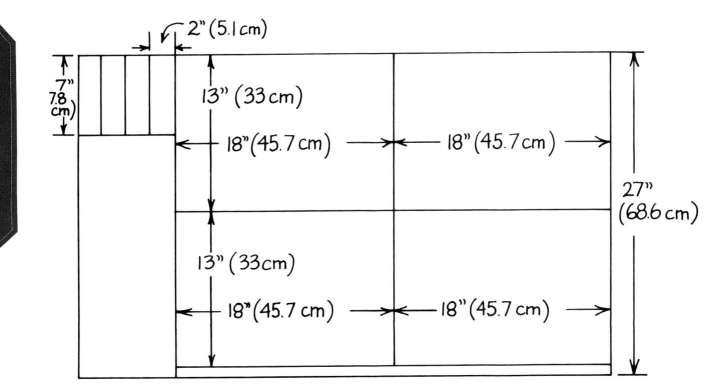

2" (5.1 cm)

7"
7.8
cm)

13" (33 cm)

18" (45.7 cm)   18" (45.7 cm)

27"
(68.6 cm)

13" (33 cm)

18" (45.7 cm)   18" (45.7 cm)

FIGURE 2

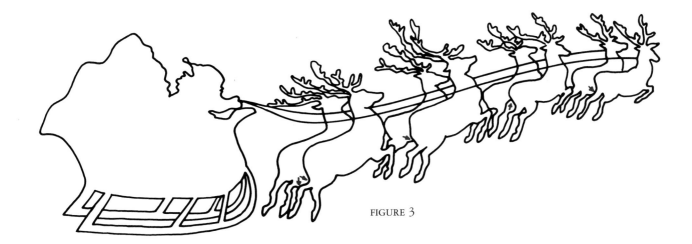

FIGURE 3

EMBROIDERED TABLECLOTH AND NAPKINS

For a truly elegant table setting, Mary Savage designed this richly embroidered tablecloth and coordinated napkins.

The embroidered figure may be placed on opposite corners or on all four to create a treasured family heirloom.

MATERIALS & TOOLS

- solid-colored tablecloth and napkins or sufficient fabric for your table
- tracing wheel and paper or iron-on transfer pen
- embroidery needles
- embroidery hoop
- **floss for each Santa:**
  3 skeins red DMC #321
  3 skeins ecru
  1 skein blue #311
  1 skein green #699
  1 skein purple #550
  1 skein pink #961
  1 skein flesh #3774
  1 skein gray #317
  1 skein black #310
- short lengths of blue and purple ribbon ⅛" (3 mm) wide

INSTRUCTIONS

1 ▪ If you're not using an existing tablecloth, begin by cutting the fabric to fit your table and the desired number of 18" (45.7-cm) squares for napkins. Turn and hem all the raw edges.

2 ▪ Enlarge *figure 1* to the desired size and trace it onto your tablecloth. Trace the design on all four corners or on two opposite corners as desired.

3 ▪ For all of the embroidery, use three strands of floss unless otherwise indicated.

4 ▪ Begin the face by outlining the eyes, nose, cheeks, and eyebrows in gray stitching. Fill in the cheeks with pink; then complete the rest of the face with short stitches in flesh tone, angling the stitches to emphasize the shapes of the facial features. Using a single strand of black floss, outline the eyeballs and eyes, and add lines to the eyebrows.

5 ▪ Fill the entire area of the mittens with French knots, placing them very close together. Then outline the edge of the top mitten with a line of black stitches.

6 ▪ Using six strands of floss, fill in the packages with long satin stitches. Using a single strand of a contrasting color, stitch tiny Xs over the surface to add designs and hold the satin stitches. Use pink on the purple package, purple on the green package, and ecru on the blue package.

7 ▪ Outline the mustache in ecru; then fill in with long and short stitches. After stitching the lower lip in pink, fill in the beard with long and short stitches in ecru.

8 ▪ Use ecru to outline the cuff of the hat. Then fill the area with long and short stitches that go back and forth horizontally across the cuff. When the entire area is solidly filled, add more ecru stitches in random directions over the surface. Allow some of the stitches to extend beyond the border so that the cuff has a furry appearance rather than a smooth edge. Repeat this technique with the cuffs on the sleeves.

9 ▪ In red floss, outline the outside edges of the sleeves and top portion of the hat. Fill in both areas with long and short stitches.

10 ▪ Finish the point of the hat by stitching a star design in ecru, as shown in the photograph.

11 ▪ Make tiny bows with the ribbons and secure them to the packages by sewing through their center knots.

12 ▪ Stitch the snowflakes using a single strand of ecru floss.

DESIGN: MARY SAVAGE
SIZE OF FIGURE: 8" x 8" (20.3 x 20.3 CM)

FIGURE 1

KEY TO CHART

1 = Red
2 = Ecru
3 = Blue
4 = Green
5 = Purple
6 = Pink
7 = Flesh
8 = Gray
9 = Black

OUTLINE CHEEKS & NOSE IN GRAY

OUTLINE MITTENS IN BLACK

DESIGN: PAT SCHEIBLE
SIZE: 22½" x 36" (57.2 x 91.4 CM)

SAINT NICK SLIPCOVERS

Whether it's a casual affair or a formal dinner party, your guests will be bowled over by these larger-than-life Santas. In this duo, designer Pat Scheible varied the materials and trim to make "his" and "hers" slipcovers.

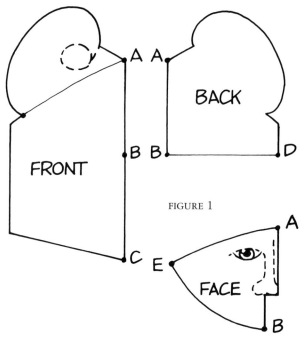

FIGURE 1

MATERIALS & TOOLS

(for each slipcover)

- approximately 1¾ yds. (1.6 m) heavy velveteen, corduroy, or plush
- polyester batting
- fusible fleece or compressed batting
- approximately ¾ yd. (68.6 cm) suede cloth
- color-coordinated sewing thread
- sewing machine
- glue gun
- 1 lb. (454 g) cotton roving or heavy white yarn
- old fur collar or strip of artificial fur
- black and green permanent markers
- pressed powder blush

INSTRUCTIONS

1 • Modify the patterns in *figure 1* to conform to the measurements of your dining chairs and make a template of each. In the figure, AB is the height of the chair back above the seat; AC is the total height of the chair; BD is the width of the chair back plus 1½" (3.8 cm).

2 • Cut a front and a back and turn up the hems. Stitch them together, leaving the bottom open. Then test the fit on your chairs.

3 • Stiffen the hat section by inserting one piece of fusible fleece and one piece of batting (both cut to fit the hat area minus the seam allowances) and stitch through all layers on the dotted line in the pattern.

4 • Before cutting the face, prepare the fabric. Wet the suede cloth and crumple it into a ball to dry. This gives Santa his wrinkles.

5 • Cut two face shapes from the crumpled suede cloth. With right sides together, stitch the two pieces, leaving an opening in the hairline. Turn the face right side out, stuff it lightly with polyester batting, and stitch on the dotted line. Then hot-glue it to the slipcover.

6 • Glue the cotton roving in place for the beard, mustache, hair, and eyebrows. Add the fur trim to the hat and glue some artificial fruit on the fur for an accent.

7 • Using the stitching as a guide, draw an eye with the permanent markers. Then give Santa a rosy glow by adding some blush to the cheeks.

DESIGN: MARY PARKER
SIZE: 4½" x 18" (11.4 x 45.7 CM)

SANTA WINE BOTTLE COVERS

The customary bottle of wine assumes a greater significance when it's presented in this cheery Santa cover designed by Mary Parker. After the contents have been consumed, your host can replace the bottle in its cover and display it as a holiday decoration.

MATERIALS & TOOLS

- ⅓ yd. (30.5 cm) red fabric
- ¼ yd. (22.9 cm) white fabric
- ⅓ yd. (30.5 cm) flesh-colored fabric
- ⅓ yd. (30.5 cm) paper-backed fusible web
- ½ yd. (45.7 cm) ⅜" (1-cm) elastic
- sewing thread
- white rayon or high-gloss cotton decorative thread
- decorative thread in desired eye color
- decorative thread one shade darker than chosen skin tone
- pompon

INSTRUCTIONS

1 ▪ From the red fabric, cut a triangle with a curved base and a rectangle according to *figure 1*. Then cut two rectangles from the white fabric as shown in *figure 2*. Cut a rectangle 9" x 12" (22.9 x 30.5 cm) from the skin-tone fabric.

2 ▪ Cut a piece of fusible web 5½" x 12" (14 x 30.5 cm) and place it on the wrong side of the red rectangle, matching both short edges and one long edge. Cut a second piece of bonding web the same size as the larger white rectangle and place it on the wrong side of the fabric. Fuse both pieces.

3 ▪ Place the red rectangle with the bonding web facing up and mark the center point of the long edge on the bonding web. Measure 4½" (11.4 cm) down from the mark and make an X. As shown in *figure 3*, draw a line from the X to the two corners. Then cut out the triangular piece.

4 ▪ Enlarge the pattern in *figure 4* and transfer the dotted lines to the white bonded fabric. Taking care not to cut off Santa's mustache, cut along the dotted lines.

5 ▪ Place the red rectangle on top of the skin-tone rectangle, matching the bottom edges, and fuse them together. There will be a strip 1½" (3.8 cm) at the bottom that isn't bonded, and the flesh-colored fabric will overextend the red fabric at the top.

6 ▪ Matching the top and side edges, lay the cut piece of white fabric on top of the skin-tone fabric. The white beard/hair will slightly overlap the red fabric already attached. Fuse.

7 ▪ Outline Santa's face, mustache, and hair/beard with satin stitch using decorative white thread. If desired, use a decorative stitch to suggest the texture of Santa's hair and beard. Then machine-embroider Santa's eyes and nose in appropriate colors.

8 ▪ Cut two eyebrows from white fabric and fuse them in place. Then satin-stitch around the edges.

9 ▪ With right sides together, sew the two shorter ends of the Santa cover together with a ½" (1.3-cm) seam. Press the seam open.

10 ▪ Fold the triangle for the cap with right sides together and sew a ½" (1.3-cm) seam along the side edges.

11 ▪ With right sides facing *out*, fold the hat band lengthwise. Press the fold to make a crease; then open the band. With right sides together, match the shorter ends and sew a ½" (1.3-cm) seam. Press open.

12 ▪ Refold the hat band lengthwise on the crease. Matching the raw edges, pin the band to the right side of the hat. Sew a ½" (1.3-cm) seam.

13 ▪ Place the hat and band assembly inside the Santa cover, matching all the raw edges. The right side of the Santa cover should face the hat band, which should face the right side of the hat. Sew a ½" (1.3-cm) seam. Press the completed seam toward the hat.

14 ▪ Around the bottom edge of the cover, press under ½" (1.3 cm) of the unbonded fabric. Overcast the edge with a zigzag stitch, leaving a small opening to insert the elastic. Then insert the elastic and adjust it so that it will hold the cover in place but isn't too tight to allow the wine bottle to be inserted.

15 ▪ Turn the cover right side out and sew the pompon onto the top of Santa's hat.

FIGURE 1

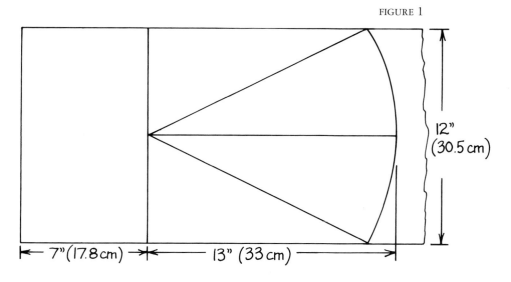

← 7" (17.8 cm) → ← 13" (33 cm) → 12" (30.5 cm)

FIGURE 2

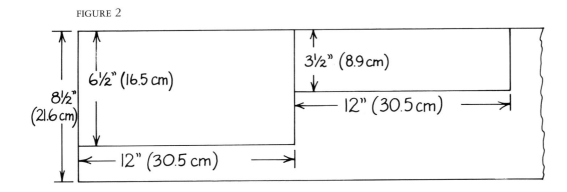

6½" (16.5 cm)

3½" (8.9 cm)

8½" (21.6 cm)

12" (30.5 cm)

12" (30.5 cm)

FIGURE 3

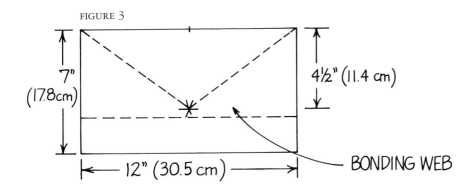

7" (17.8 cm)

4½" (11.4 cm)

12" (30.5 cm)

BONDING WEB

FIGURE 4

DESIGN: MARY PARKER
SIZE: 18" x 15" (45.7 x 38.1)

SANTA TOTE BAG

This appliquéd tote bag, designed by Mary Parker, is as practical as it is festive. It's equally handy for picking up those last-minute gifts and items at the grocery store or for delivering home-baked goodies to your host and hostess.

MATERIALS & TOOLS

- ½ yd. (45.7 cm) sturdy cotton fabric
- ½ yd. (45.7 cm) seasonal print fabric
- ¼ yd. (22.9 cm) red fabric
- ¼ yd. (22.9 cm) green fabric
- scraps of white, black, skin tone, and print fabrics
- 3 yds. (2.7 m) black webbing
- ⅛ yd. (11.4 cm) grosgrain ribbon
- ¼ yd. (22.9 cm) paper-backed fusible web
- sewing thread
- decorative rayon thread in various colors
- sewing machine

INSTRUCTIONS

1 ▪ Trim the cotton fabric to 36¾" x 18" (93.3 x 45.7 cm). Using straight pins, mark a 12" (30.5-cm) square that will be the design area on the front of the tote. Refer to *figure 1* for placement.

2 ▪ Before tracing the appliqué pieces (*fig. 2*) onto the fusible web, reverse the patterns by holding the designs up to a sunny window and tracing them onto the back of the paper. Fuse the web to the motif fabrics and trace the reversed designs onto the backing. Extend the edges of the underlying pieces so the pieces will overlap slightly.

3 ▪ Cut the designs from the bonded fabric, peel off the backing, and position them as desired. Remove the pins marking your design area; then press the motifs in place.

4 ▪ Outline each design piece with satin stitching in matching decorative thread. Then stitch the garland on the tree with gold metallic thread.

5 ▪ Cut three rectangles from the cotton rectangle as shown in *figure 3*. Note the location of the bottom and side seams and mark the center bottom seam as shown.

6 ▪ Place the right sides of the tote together and sew the side and bottom seams with a ⅜" (1-cm) allowance. This will leave two unjoined areas at the bottom corners of your tote (*fig. 4*). Insert both index fingers into one of these corners and pull the fabric taut so that the unsewn portion from the bottom meets that from the side. Pin this in place; then sew a ⅜" (1-cm) seam. Repeat on the other corner.

7 ▪ At the top of the tote, turn under 2½" (6.4 cm) of fabric to the inside (wrong side). Press but don't sew.

8 ▪ Cut the webbing into two equal lengths. With the tote still inside-out, shape one piece of webbing into a U and tuck each end into the seam allowance at the bottom of the tote, placing each end 4" (10.2 cm) from the center of the bottom seam. Don't twist the webbing; the same side should be pinned at both ends. Continue pinning the webbing against the wrong side of the tote fabric in parallel lines up to the edge of the hem at the top. Allow enough ease in the webbing that it doesn't pull the tote fabric. When you reach the hem on each side, pin the webbing only to the hem, not through to the outer fabric. Release all of the pins except those holding the webbing to the hem. Then repeat on the other side of the tote with the second piece of webbing.

9 ▪ Stitch the webbing only to the hem area on both sides of the tote. Then hand-baste the ends of the webbing back under the seam allowance at the bottom.

10 ▪ Cut the lining fabric as shown in *figure 2*, but decrease the length from 18" (45.7 cm) to 13¾" (34.9 cm). With right sides together, start at the top and sew 3" (7.6 cm) of the side seam with a ⅜" (1-cm) seam allowance. Press the seam open and turn the lining right side out.

FIGURE 1

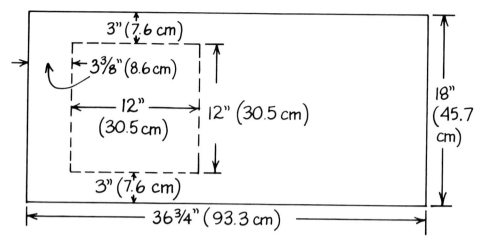

3" (7.6 cm)

3⅜" (8.6 cm)

12" (30.5 cm)

12" (30.5 cm)

3" (7.6 cm)

18" (45.7 cm)

36¾" (93.3 cm)

FIGURE 2

FIGURE 3

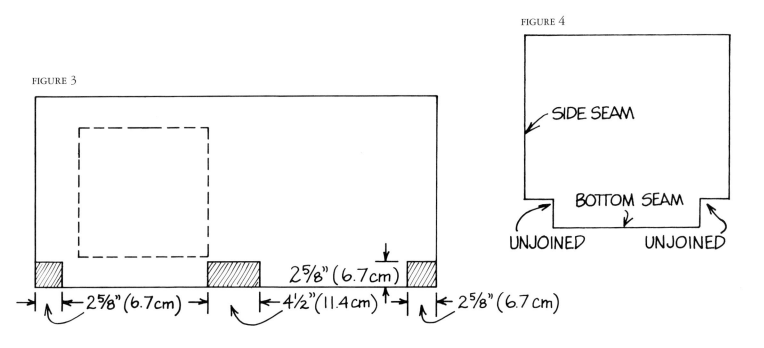

2⅝" (6.7 cm)

|←— 2⅝" (6.7cm) —→| |←— 4½" (11.4 cm) →| |←— 2⅝" (6.7 cm) →|

FIGURE 4

← SIDE SEAM

BOTTOM SEAM

UNJOINED   UNJOINED

11. With the right sides of the tote and lining together, match the seams. Align the raw edges along the top of the tote and lining and sew a ⅜" (1-cm) seam. Press the seam toward the lining.

12. Turn the lining; then with the right sides together, stitch 3" (7.6 cm) of the side seam from the bottom corner. Press open. Pull the bottom of the lining through the unsewn middle area of the side seam and with the right sides together, stitch the bottom seam. Then stitch the open corners as you did for the tote in step 6.

13. Turn the lining right side out and fit it into the tote. Hand-baste the bottom seams of the tote and lining together.

14. Open the tote and stand it upright. With a piece of chalk, mark the area that forms the bottom of the tote. Hand-baste the webbing in place where it crosses under the chalk line; then stitch over the chalk line on your machine. Also stitch ¼" (6 mm) on each side of the center seam. This will secure the handles and ensure that the lining and tote stay together.

15. Slip-stitch the side seam of the lining completely closed.

CHEF CLAUS APRON

Whipping up holiday delicacies is much more enjoyable with Chef Santa right there to lend moral support and protect you from spills. This festive apron, designed by Mary Parker, is reversible; on the other side is a festive holiday print.

MATERIALS & TOOLS

- 1 yd. (91.4 cm) medium- to heavy-weight solid-colored background fabric
- 1 yd. seasonal print lining fabric
- 7" x 14" (17.8 x 35.6 cm) red fabric
- 4" x 12" (10.2 x 30.5 cm) white fabric
- 4" x 5" (10.2 x 12.7 cm) black fabric
- 3" x 3" (7.6 x 7.6 cm) skin-tone fabric
- 1" x 4" (2.5 x 10.2 cm) print fabric
- ⅓ yd. (30.5 cm) paper-backed fusible web
- sewing thread to match background fabric
- spools of decorative thread in assorted colors
- scissors
- sewing machine

INSTRUCTIONS

1 • Using the measurements shown in *figure 1*, cut one piece for the body of the apron from both the background fabric and the lining. Cut two pieces from each fabric measuring 2" x 30" (5.1 x 76.2 cm) for the ties and one piece measuring 2" x 22" (5.1 x 55.9 cm) for the neck band.

2 • Enlarge the pattern in *figure 2* and make a template. Cut the template apart to make separate pattern pieces for each color for Santa and the cake and plate.

3 • Following the manufacturer's instructions, apply the bonding web to the wrong side of the fabric pieces. Make sure to leave the paper on one side of the bonding web. Except for Santa's face, pin the patterns to the appropriate fabrics and cut out the pieces. For Santa's face, cut the fabric slightly larger than the area that will ultimately show (cut enough to include a mouth).

4 • Remove the paper backing from the cut pieces and assemble them in the center on the right side of the background fabric. Position the piece for Santa's face first; then add the clothing pieces over it. Don't place the cake or plate on the apron yet.

5 • Bond the face and clothing pieces to the apron according to the manufacturer's guidelines.

6 • Secure the edges with a decorative satin stitch all around. Mark Santa's eyebrows, eyes, and nose with decorative thread. Outline his arms and mark the contours of his jacket, hat, pants, and boots.

7 • Position the cake on its plate and place the assembly on the design so that Santa appears to be presenting the cake. Bond these pieces and secure the edges with satin stitch.

8 • Using one piece of background fabric and one of lining for each pair, pin together the right sides of the two apron ties and the neck band. Stitch a ½" (1.3-cm) seam down one long side of each piece, pivot at the corners, and continue down the other long side. Trim the seam allowance and the corners before turning the pieces right side out. Press; then top-stitch all around.

9 • With the right sides together, pin the apron body, leaving a 6" (15.2-cm) area open at the center bottom. (You'll need this area free to turn the apron.) At the appropriate places, insert the two apron ties (points marked A in figure 1) and the neck band (point B). The raw ends of the ties and neck band should be even with the raw edges of the two apron fabrics, with the entire length of the ties and band hanging loose inside the pinned area.

10 • Stitch a ½" (1.3-cm) seam all around the apron, beginning 3" (7.6 cm) in from the center of the bottom of the apron and continuing up the side to the center front. Then turn over the apron and follow the same procedure on the unsewn side. This method prevents you from having an unsightly pleat at the bottom of the lining after you turn it.

11 • Trim the seams and clip the curves. Then turn the apron right side out through the opening at the bottom. Press and topstitch all around. Sew several buttons on the end of the neck band to accommodate various chefs. Then make a matching buttonhole on the top edge of the apron front.

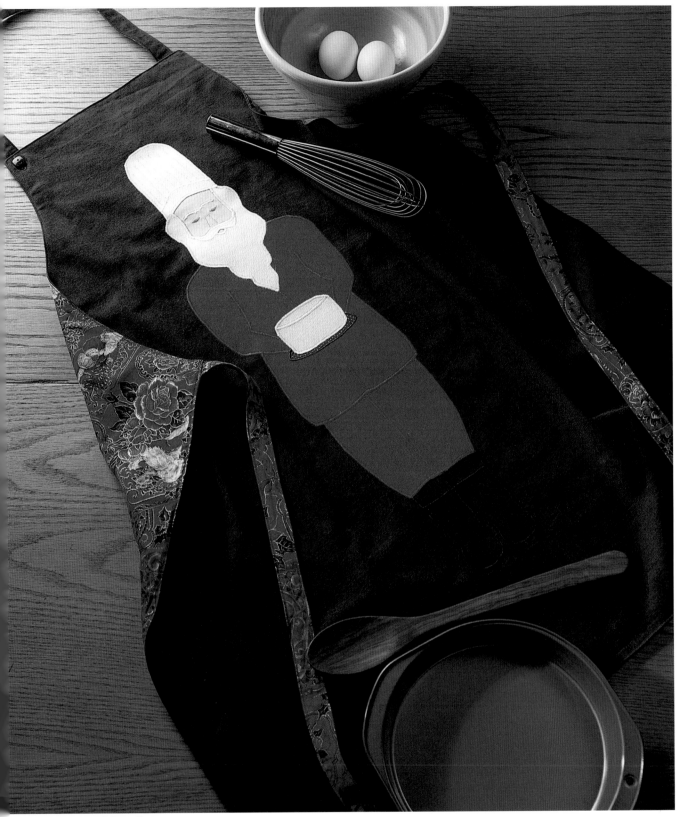

DESIGN: Mary Parker

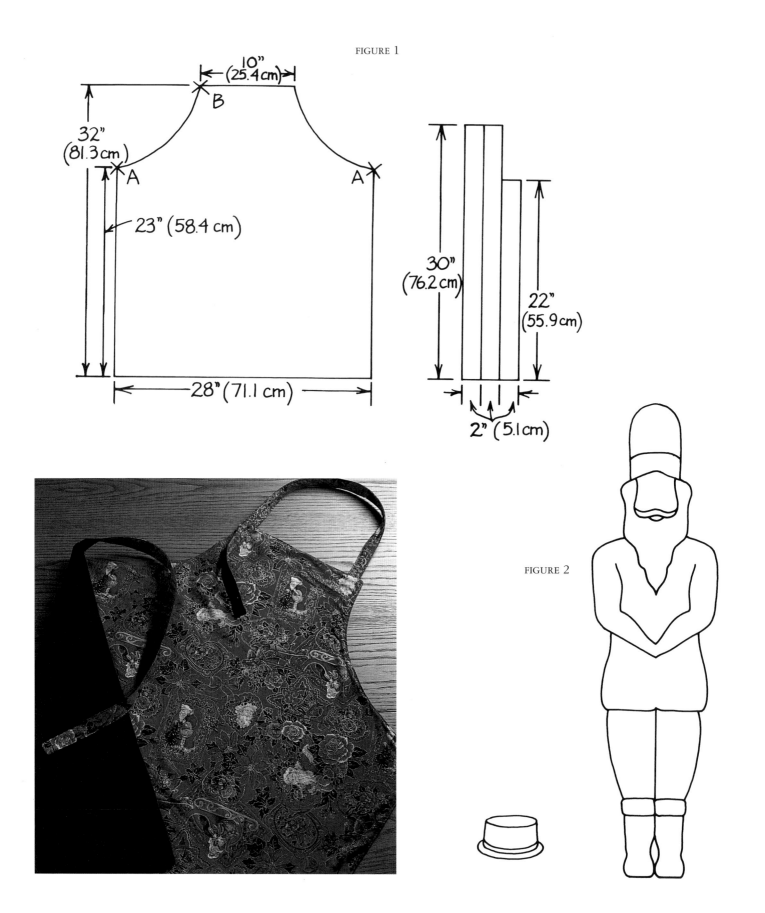

FIGURE 1

10"
(25.4 cm)

B

32"
(81.3 cm)

A   A

23" (58.4 cm)

28" (71.1 cm)

30"
(76.2 cm)

22"
(55.9 cm)

2" (5.1 cm)

FIGURE 2

DESIGN: LULA CHANG AND CATHI ROSENGREN

SIZE: 4⅜" x 5" (11.1 x 12.7 CM),
DESIGN AREA

INTER WONDERLAND SANTA

This delightful piece is the result of a collaborative effort; Lula Chang painted the needlepoint design, and Cathi Rosengren stitched the pattern and made it into a candy holder.

It would be equally striking as a framed wall hanging, throw pillow, or small handbag.

MATERIALS & TOOLS

- 18-mesh canvas
- tapestry needle
- laying tool
- *Rainbow Gallery* (1 skein each)
  Splendor S859
  Neon Rays N55
  Rainbow Linen R457, R455
  Wisper W98, W88
  Cresta d'Oro C22, C10, C04
  Flair F529, F502
  Tiara T101
- *Anchor* (1 skein each)
  embroidery floss 1, 892, 882, 894, 403
- *Renaissance Designs* (1 skein each)
  Sprinkles 16, 28, 23, 02, 22, 05
- *DMC* (1 skein each)
  Medici 8993, 8897, 8381

INSTRUCTIONS

Trace the photograph of the painted canvas to create your pattern. Most of the stitches used here can be found in needlepoint books. Those that are less common are shown in *figure 1*.

MOON

Using a single strand of Sprinkles 05, outline the moon in continental stitch. Fill in the center with Sprinkles 02, using continental or basketweave stitch.

SKY

Execute double brick stitch over six threads using 6-ply Splendor S859 (to make it easier to control the tension, use 3-ply doubled). Use a laying tool while stitching to make sure your threads lie perfectly flat. Once the sky is complete, use Tiara T101 to add the gold accents as shown.

SNOW

Stitch the snow with double cross stitch. The bottom cross of the stitch is done in the color indicated on the painted canvas (either Sprinkles 28 or 16), and the top cross is always done in Sprinkles 28.

TREES

Using 2-ply Medici 8897, fill in the trees with long random stitches. Work downward from the top of the tree and flare the stitches outward.

FACE

Stitch the face in embroidery floss as painted, using continental or basketweave stitch. For the eyebrows, use 2-ply Medici 8381, working random stitches to mimic real hair.

BEARD

With one strand each of Wisper W98 and W88 in the same needle, make long vertical stitches from the hat to the collar, then from below the moustache to the collar. In the portion of the beard under the moustache, place some French knots using the same fibers.

MOUSTACHE

With the same fibers used for the beard, complete the moustache in bullion stitch.

BASKET

The body of the basket is done in burden stitch (refer to the chart in *figure 1*). Thread two needles, one with Rainbow Linen R455 and one with Rainbow Linen R457. You will be doubling this fiber (making it 2 ply), so make sure that your thread is long enough. With R457, place the vertical stitch between the third and fourth thread from the left side of the basket, beginning at the top of the basket and following along in the "trench" between the third and fourth thread to the bottom of the basket. You now have one long stitch. Using the other needle and R455, make a horizontal stitch covering six threads, with the long vertical stitch in the center. Make a second horizontal stitch in the trench below the first one. Skip two trenches and stitch again. As shown in the chart, make subsequent burden stitches so that the horizontal portions are offset, creating a basket-weave effect.

Stitch the handle in lazy daisy stitch, using a single ply of Rainbow Linen R455. Work from left to right as pictured. Using continental or basketweave stitch, complete the items in the basket with Sprinkles 23, 22, and 05.

SANTA'S GARMENTS

Outline all areas of the coat in continental stitch using Tiara T101. For the collar, use alternating colors of Cresta d'Oro C10 and C22 in Scotch stitch. Complete the coat in small grounding stitch (see the chart), using Neon Rays N55 and embellishing it with Tiara T101. Stitch the top portion of the hat in small grounding stitch also. On the hat band, use 3-ply Medici 8993 to do cut turkey tufting. Stitch the shoes in basketweave with Cresta d'Oro C10. Use a combination of stitches for the gloves. First use Cresta d'Oro 04 to do a large cross stitch across four canvas threads. Then, in the open area, make a small upright cross stitch using 6-ply Anchor floss 403 (see the chart).

CANDY CANE

Using Flair 529 and 502, make diagonal flat stitches from the lower left to the upper right, turning as necessary to emulate a candy cane.

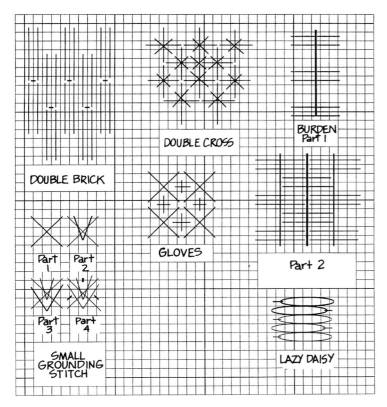

FIGURE 1

ANTA'S GYM BASEBALL CAP

It's very strenuous work delivering presents all over the world on a single night, and all of Santa's helpers need to stay in shape. This fanciful cap, created by Pat Scheible and her goddaughter, Sythong Vannavong, is a must-wear to one of your holiday parties.

MATERIALS & TOOLS

- small figurines in tumbling positions
- acrylic paints
- artist's brush
- small piece of clear acetate
- silver metallic tape
- white baseball cap
- glue gun
- 400 white pompons
- miniature trees
- red braided cord
- small piece of lightweight cardboard
- permanent markers

INSTRUCTIONS

1 • Paint the figurines to look like Santas and set them aside to dry.

2 • Cut rectangular pieces of clear acetate to use for doors, adding strips of metallic tape around the edges to simulate metal framing. Hot-glue the outside edges of the doors to the front of the baseball cap.

3 • Using a dab of hot glue for each one, attach the pompons to the cap in rows. Place the first row adjacent to the doors and continue back until the entire crown is covered. Glue an additional row onto the front of the doors to give them an entryway reminiscent of an igloo.

4 • Position the trees and figures onto the bill of the cap and hot-glue them in place.

5 • Complete the cap by gluing a piece of braided cord onto the edge of the bill and placing a cardboard sign over the door.

DESIGN: PAT SCHEIBLE
SIZE: 9" x 4" (22.9 x 10.2 CM)

JUST FOR FUN

SANTA HAND PUPPET

One of the easiest ways to create a professional-looking hand puppet is to use a small gourd for the head. Ginger Summit, an accomplished gourd artist, has incorporated the protruding stem end of the gourd to give this Santa a nose worthy of Jimmy Durante.

DESIGN: GINGER SUMMIT
SIZE: 12½" x 21" (31.8 x 53.3 CM)

MATERIALS & TOOLS

- small hard-shell gourd, cured and cleaned
- acrylic or tempera paints
- small paintbrush
- newspaper
- sewing thread
- sewing machine
- scrap of black fabric
- ⅓ yd. (30.5 cm) red fabric
- ¼ yd. (22.9 cm) polyester fleece
- electric drill with ¼" (6-mm) and ¹⁄₁₆" (1.6-mm) bits
- white glue
- metal skewer
- unspun wool fleece
- sharp knife
- keyhole saw
- curved tapestry needle
- heavy-gauge thread

INSTRUCTIONS

1 ▪ Apply a base coat of acrylic paint to the gourd and allow it to dry.

2 ▪ After mixing the desired skin tone, paint the face area of the gourd. Use a mixture of pinks to give Santa his rosy glow. Allow the paint to dry; then add the eyes.

3 ▪ Using your own hand and arm to determine the measurements, draw a simple pattern for the robe on the newspaper (see *figure 1*). As a general guideline, the length of the fabric from the neck to the hem should be about 12" (30.5 cm), and you should allow about 3" (7.6 cm) for the neck to be attached to the puppet head. The distance between the puppet hands should be about 8" (20.3 cm). Before cutting the fabric, make sure the dimensions of your pattern fit both your hand and the puppet head. Don't forget to add a seam allowance of at least ¼" (6 mm) and a hem of about 1" (2.5 cm).

4 ▪ Cut two pieces of fabric for the robe and sew the shoulder and side seams. Then hem the bottom. Cut two narrow bands of polyester fleece and stitch them to the sleeves to make cuffs.

5 ▪ The hat is a semicircle of red fabric. Again make a newspaper pattern, drawing the semicircle to fit your gourd. Then cut the fabric and sew it into a cone. Add a band of polyester fleece around the bottom.

6 ▪ Cut two pieces for each mitten from the black fabric. After sewing the pieces together, turn the mittens right side out and attach them to the sleeves of the robe.

7 ▪ Using the ¼" (6-mm) bit, drill holes in all of the areas of the gourd where the hair and beard will be attached.

8 ▪ Put a dab of glue in one of the holes and use a skewer to push one end of a small amount of unspun wool fleece into the hole. Continue to fill all the holes with bits of wool. When all the hair is in place, let the glue dry completely.

9 ▪ Use the keyhole saw to cut a hole at the bottom of Santa's head, making the hole large enough to insert at least two fingers. Clean out all the seeds and pulp. Then drill ¹⁄₁₆" (1.6-mm) holes around the large hole, spacing them about 1" (2.5 cm) apart.

10 ▪ Using heavy-duty thread and a curved tapestry needle, stitch the robe onto the gourd through the small holes. Further anchor the fabric to the gourd with glue if desired.

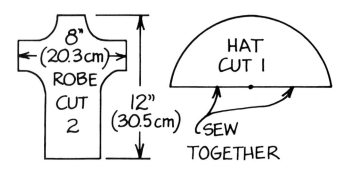

FIGURE 1

OMERSAULTING SANTA

Simple toys are fun to make, and a tumbling Santa is certain to bring plenty of laughter to your holiday celebrations. To demonstrate how you might customize the decoration of your own Santa, designer Terry Taylor created two versions of this squeeze toy.

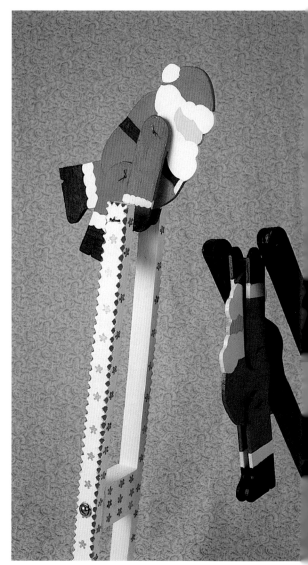

DESIGN: TERRY TAYLOR
SIZE: 3" x 16" (7.6 x 40.6 CM)

MATERIALS & TOOLS

- 2 pieces ½" x ¹¹⁄₁₆" x 16" (1.3 x 1.7 x 40.6 cm) pine or basswood
- 1 sheet ⅛" x 4" x 24" (0.3 x 10.2 x 61 cm) basswood
- ½" x 1¾" x 1⅜" (1.3 x 4.4 x 3.5 cm) block of pine or basswood
- ⅛" dia. x ½" (0.3 x 1.5 cm) dowel
- acrylic paints
- ¼" (6-mm) soft brush
- 1" (2.5-cm) foam brush
- clear acrylic spray sealer
- gold stamp pad
- pencil with unused eraser
- electric drill with ¹⁄₁₆" (2-mm) and ⅛" (3-mm) bits
- motorized "mini-tool" or jigsaw
- ⅛" x 3" (0.3 x 7.6 cm) bolt, washer, nut, and finish washer
- pocketknife or carving knife
- 24" (61 cm) small-gauge copper or steel wire
- needle-nose pliers
- wire cutters
- small c-clamp
- 24" (61 cm) heavy carpet thread

INSTRUCTIONS

1 ▪ Trace the pattern for the Santa figure onto the sheet of basswood and cut one body, two arms, and two legs using a motorized "mini-tool" or jigsaw. Sand all edges and surfaces and set aside.

2 ▪ Mark the positions of the holes on the arms, body, and legs. Then, using a ¹⁄₁₆" (2-mm) bit, drill holes through the pieces.

3 ▪ Sand all surfaces of the two 16" (40.6-cm) pieces of wood. These are Santa's supports. Measure ½" (1.3 cm) down from one end of each support and center two marks spaced about ¼" (6 mm) apart on the ¹¹⁄₁₆" (1.7-cm) face. Using the ¹⁄₁₆" bit, drill two holes on each piece as marked.

4 ▪ Measure 9¼" (23.5 cm) down from the end where you just drilled the two holes and center a mark. Use the ⅛" (3-mm) bit to drill a hole at the mark. Repeat this on the second support.

5 ▪ An optional decoration is to chip-carve the edges of the supports. Use a knife to make small V-cuts all along the edges.

6 ▪ Mark the center on the 1⅜" (3.5-cm) side of the small block. Using the ⅛" bit, drill a hole through the block at the mark.

7 ▪ Apply a base coat of acrylic paint to all the pieces and allow them to dry.

8 ▪ Using a pencil, lightly draw the outlines for the face, beard, boot, gloves, and belt onto the figure pieces. Then paint the features on all sides of the pieces as indicated, allowing them to dry between coats.

9 ▪ When the paint is dry, spray a light coat of the acrylic sealer on one side of each piece. Allow the sealer to dry before spraying the other side.

10 ▪ If you've chip-carved the edges of the supports, use a small brush and paint each V-cut. Allow it to dry.

11 ▪ Use the foam brush to paint the supports and the center block. By lightly applying the foam brush to each surface you will leave the small V-cuts untouched, revealing the contrasting color. Allow the paint to dry and apply a second coat if needed.

12 ▪ Draw a small star shape on the unused eraser. Using a craft knife, trim away the excess eraser around the star to make a rubber stamp.

13 ▪ Experiment with the cut eraser and a gold metallic stamp pad to determine how much to ink your rubber stamp. When satisfied with the results, decorate the supports as desired. Allow the ink to dry thoroughly before spraying it with acrylic sealer.

14 ▪ Cut four 2" (5.1-cm) lengths of wire. Using needle-nose pliers, twist two lengths together in the center for about ⅜" (1 cm). Repeat with the remaining two lengths.

15 ▪ Use the twisted wires to attach the arms and legs to the body. Thread one pair of wires through the top body hole, then through one arm on each side. Spread the ends of the wire apart to hold the arms in place. Repeat with the legs at the bottom hole. Trim the ends of the wire to about ¼" (6 mm). Your figure should move smoothly.

16 ▪ Paint the small dowel to match Santa's gloves. After the paint has dried, carefully apply glue to the ends of the dowel and place it between and slightly below the drilled holes of the gloves. Carefully clamp the assembly and allow the glue to dry.

17 ▪ Thread the bolt through the finish nut, the bottom hole in one support, the center block, and the second support. Finish with the small washer and nut.

18 ▪ Cut the carpet thread in half and thread each length through the small holes in the supports and through Santa's gloves. Tie off the ends securely.

19 ▪ Grasp the ends of the supports and give a gentle squeeze. As you continue to squeeze, Santa will begin to somersault!

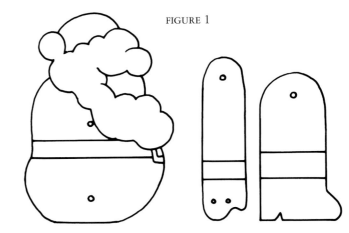

FIGURE 1

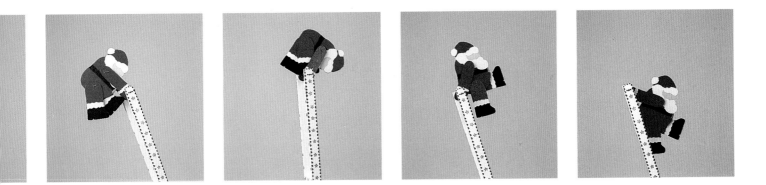

DESIGN: BEVERLY ROBBINS
SIZE: 7" x 11" (17.8 x 27.9 CM)

ANTA CAT GOURD

As befits the regal nature of a feline, these cat Santas are garbed in the robe and miter of an Old World Saint Nicholas. Each of Beverly Robbins' hand-painted Santas is in complete control of his holiday tasks, as demonstrated by how firmly he grasps his tail.

MATERIALS & TOOLS

- bottle gourd, cured and cleaned
- acrylic paints
- transfer pen and paper
- small, medium, and large flat brushes
- artist's brushes
- spray matte acrylic sealer
- wood putty
- waxed paper
- palette knife
- sandpaper
- carpenter's wood glue

INSTRUCTIONS

1 • Apply a base coat of acrylic paint to the entire gourd, choosing a color that will be prominent in your final design (rose or brick red in these two pieces).

2 • After the base coat has dried, enlarge the designs in *figure 1* to fit your gourd and transfer them to the surface. Alternatively, use a pencil to sketch a Santa design that incorporates your family pet. This is easier if you work from a photograph than from the live subject.

3 • No matter what type of animal you're painting, begin with the face. You can adjust the hat and coat as needed to fit around the edges of the face. The face is also

the most detailed area of the design. Blend your colors as you paint to give your results a more natural appearance and to avoid hard edges.

4 • Paint the hat and coat as shown. To avoid a high-waisted look, place the bottom edge of the coat near the bottom of the gourd. Don't forget to leave room for the tail. Paint the arms and mittened paws next. Add the tail in a smooth curve from the back of the gourd to the mitten on one paw.

5 • After the paint has dried, protect the surface with two coats of spray matte sealer.

6 • Mix the wood putty by gradually adding small amounts of water to form a workable ball. Form the putty into an oblong mass and place it on the waxed paper. Then center the painted gourd over the putty and press down lightly. Use a palette knife to shape the putty into two boots. Let the putty dry before removing it from the gourd.

7 • When the boots have dried completely, sand them lightly and paint them. Attach the boots to the bottom of the gourd with wood glue.

8 • After the piece has dried for at least 24 hours, apply three or four additional coats of spray matte sealer.

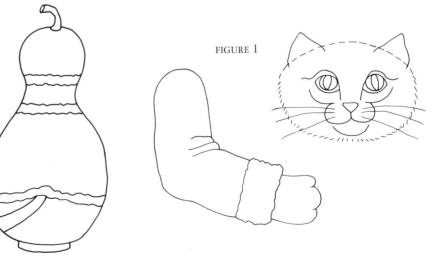

FIGURE 1

TAR-SURFING SANTA

According to Marj Beaty, Santa has to keep pace with all the latest developments in recreational gear so that he can keep his lists of toys up to date. Here she's captured him in the act of testing out some surfing equipment; it looks as though he just caught a blast of solar wind.

MATERIALS & TOOLS

- ¼ yd. (22.9 cm) cotton print
- ⅜ yd. (34.3 cm) muslin
- ⅛ yd. (11.4 cm) stretchy swimsuit fabric
- ⅛ yd. (11.4 cm) complementary cotton print
- scraps of bright yellow and blue fabrics
- sewing thread
- decorative thread in assorted colors
- sewing machine
- polyester fiberfill
- fabric paint pens (optional)
- soft red pencil
- lamb's wool
- glue gun
- ⅛"-dia. (3-mm) dowel 10" (25.4 cm) long
- 18-gauge floral wire 18" (45.7 cm) long
- gold acrylic paint
- ¼ yd. (22.9 cm) paper-backed fusible web
- gold glitter spray
- 3 yds. (2.7 m) gold cord

DESIGN: MARJORIE INGALLS BEATY
SIZE: 8½" x 11" (21.6 x 27.9 CM)

INSTRUCTIONS

1 ▪ To make the star surfboard, cut two 9" (22.9-cm) squares of cotton print fabric and align them with the right sides together. Draw an 8" (20.3-cm) star and machine-stitch the two pieces together along the lines of the star, leaving one seam open for turning. For added strength, stitch the seam a second time; then trim the seams and clip the curves. Turn and press. After filling the star with fiberfill, hand-stitch the opening closed.

2 ▪ Santa's body is approximately 5½" x 5" (14 x 12.7 cm), and the legs are 5" long. Make templates for Santa's body and legs according to the patterns in *figure 1*, adding the desired seam allowances, and cut the indicated number of pieces from the muslin. Double-stitch the seams for strength; then clip the curves and trim the seams. Turn and press.

3 ▪ Stuff Santa's body to within 1" (2.5 cm) of the open base. Fold both edges of the base inward and hand-stitch them closed. Stuff Santa's legs only up to the knees. Matching the seams, hand-stitch the legs to the base of the body. With off-white heavy thread, hand-stitch toes, fingers, wrists, and knees.

4 ▪ Cut a ½" (1.3-cm) circle of muslin for the nose. Gather it around the edge, stuff it lightly, and sew it to the face by hand. The other features can be embroidered or drawn with fabric paint pens. Use a soft red pencil to add a rosy glow to Santa's cheeks, nose, hands, knees, ankles, and tummy.

5 ▪ Tack or glue pieces of curly wool to the face and head to make Santa's beard and hair.

6 ▪ Cut a piece of stretchy fabric 4½" x 3" (11.4 x 7.6 cm). As shown in *figure 1*, fold it in half and stitch the side seam and inseam where the legs will go. Clip the curves and turn the suit right side out. Cut low armholes and a neckline. Place the suit on Santa and tack the shoulder seams to the body.

7 ▪ Wrap the floral wire onto the dowel to create a framework for the sail (*fig. 2*). Paint the dowel with gold acrylic paint.

8 ▪ Using fusible web, join two pieces of the cotton print fabric with the wrong sides together. Cut a sail about ⅛" to ¼" (3 to 6 mm) larger than the wire frame. Make sure that 2" (5.1 cm) of the dowel extends below the bottom of the sail. Using metallic gold thread, hand-stitch the sail to the dowel and wire frame.

9 ▪ Make a small hole in the center of the star and insert some hot glue. Push the dowel into the hole, securing it with additional glue.

10 ▪ Make a sun by cutting two circles from the bright yellow fabric. Placing the end of the dowel between the two pieces, glue the sun to the top of the mast.

11 ▪ Glue Santa's hand to the mast and stitch his feet to the star. A few blue stars, cut from doubled fabric and fused together, may be threaded onto a length of gold metallic thread to run from Santa's hand to the mast. If desired, spray the figure lightly with gold glitter.

12 ▪ To make your surfing Santa a hanging ornament, attach four 20" (50.8-cm) lengths of gold cord to four of the star's points, making a bow at each point. Stitch the cord securely in place at each point. Add a bow at the fifth point and tie the cords together at the top.

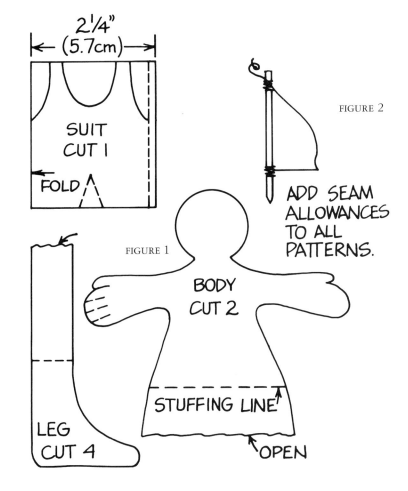

2¼" (5.7cm)

SUIT CUT 1

FOLD

FIGURE 2

ADD SEAM ALLOWANCES TO ALL PATTERNS.

FIGURE 1

BODY CUT 2

LEG CUT 4

STUFFING LINE

OPEN

 CROBATIC SANTA

As much as anyone else in this fitness-conscious world, Santa likes to display his athletic prowess. Designers Nan and Bill Parker have dressed him in a sporty gingham suit for his holiday debut on the trapeze.

DESIGN: NAN AND BILL PARKER
SIZE: 12½" x 27½" (31.8 x 69.9 CM)

MATERIALS & TOOLS

- ¾ yd. (68.6 cm) tea-dyed muslin
- ¾ yd. (68.6 cm) gingham or other cotton print
- ¼ yd. (22.9 cm) complementary trim fabric
- ¼" (6-mm) elastic
- sewing thread
- sewing machine
- scraps of felt
- 3 yds. (2.7 m) wool yarn
- small piece of cardboard
- button
- fabric paint pen
- glue gun
- basket handle or heavy copper wire and wooden spool

INSTRUCTIONS

1 ▪ From the tea-dyed muslin, cut two body pieces and four arms and legs according to the patterns in *figure 1*. Be sure to add seam allowances to all the patterns before cutting.

2 ▪ Sew the side seams on all the body parts, leaving one end open on each. Trim the seams, clip the corners, and turn the pieces right side out. After lightly stuffing each piece with fiberfill, stitch the openings closed.

3 ▪ To assemble the figure, attach the arms at the shoulders so that they extend over Santa's head. The legs hang straight down from the bottom of the body.

4 ▪ Cut the pattern pieces for the bodice, sleeves, facings, pants, and hat from the complementary fabrics, combining them as desired. Stitch the bodice front to the back at the shoulders. Then fold under the edge around the neckline and stitch a loose basting stitch. (This will be gathered later to fit the body.) Complete the bodice by sewing the side seams.

5 ▪ With the right sides together, stitch the cuff facings to the bottom edges of the sleeves. Press the facings toward the wrong sides of the sleeves; then fold under and press the raw edges of the facings. Stitch across the cuffs and facings to make a casing to hold the narrow elastic.

6 ▪ Placing the rights sides together, stitch the side seam on each sleeve, leaving an opening at the cuff to insert the elastic. Then thread pieces of elastic into the cuffs and adjust them to fit Santa's arms. Tack the openings closed with needle and thread.

7 ▪ Stitch a gathering stitch at the shoulder end of each sleeve and pull the thread gently to fit the sleeve to the armhole. Now sew the sleeves to the bodice, easing the sleeves to fit.

8 ▪ With right sides together, sew two of the pant pieces together at the crotch seam. Repeat with the other two pieces, but begin sewing 2" (5.1 cm) down from the waist. Then sew the side seams together. Fold under the bottom edges of the pant legs and sew a gathering stitch. Do the same around the waist.

9 ▪ With right sides together, align the opening in the pants with the front opening in the bodice. Then sew the pants to the bodice. Turn the suit right side out and press under the raw edges on both openings.

10 ▪ Ease the suit onto the figure and pin it to fit. Gather the neck and waist if necessary. Then stitch the openings closed by hand.

11 ▪ To make the beard, wrap wool yarn 10 times around a piece of cardboard 5" (12.7 cm) long. Using a separate piece of yarn, tie the loops together at the top. Cut them across the bottom. Then glue the yarn onto the face with hot glue.

12 ▪ Sew the two hat pieces together along the side seams; then turn the hat right side out. With the right sides together, sew the end seam of the hat band. Now fold the hat band in half lengthwise with the right side facing out. Matching the raw edges together, sew the band onto the hat. Turn the band down so that the seam faces inward and glue the hat onto Santa's head.

13 ▪ Draw the eyes on the face with a fabric marker and sew on a small button for a nose.

FIGURE 1

Enlarge all patterns by 400%

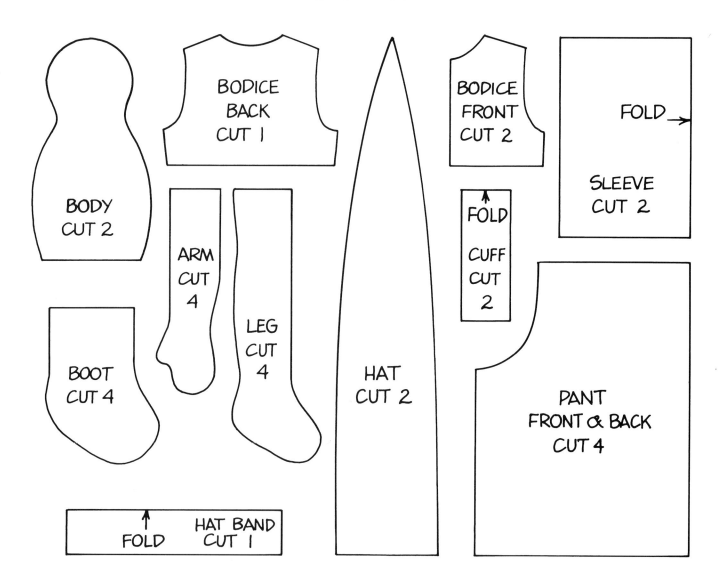

Courtesy of Fred Kahn.

ACKNOWLEDGMENTS

HEARTFELT THANKS are extended to all the talented designers represented here. Their hard work, unlimited creativity, and helpful suggestions made writing this book a pleasure. Thanks also to Fred Kahn and Terry Taylor, both of Asheville, North Carolina, for their generous loan of vintage postcards.

CONTRIBUTING DESIGNERS

MARJORIE INGALLS BEATY crafted her first doll over 20 years ago as a gift for her daughter, and she still enjoys the good humor that seems to come to life in her creations. She lives in Newbury, Massachusetts.

VIRGINIA BOEGLI began her experiments with papier-mâché 35 years ago as a tool for studying form and movement for her paintings. Since then, her pieces have ranged from inches-tall chess figures to 10-foot bronze replicas. She lives in Bozeman, Montana.

BONNIE BULLMAN has been making Santas for five years. With the help of her husband and her daughters, she collects the wood for her figures from the woods around her home. She lives in Barnardsville, North Carolina, near the Blue Ridge Parkway.

MAUREEN CARLSON'S unlimited imagination is applied to creating a world full of delightful characters through her business, Wee Folk Creations in Prior Lake, Minnesota. She recently introduced a line of press molds called What a Character, which can be used to mold a variety of human faces with polymer clay.

LULA CHANG has happily combined her passion for needlework and her vocation as an illustrator for the past 10 years. Her business, Wooly Dreams Design, in Columbia, Maryland, offers fine hand-painted needle-point canvases, cross-stitch charts, and kits.

CAROL COSTENBADER began making dolls to honor her mother, who collected boxes of antique lace, buttons, and fabrics. Trained as a sculptor in clay, she makes a porcelain head for each figure and dresses it in vintage materials. Her studio is in Asheville, North Carolina.

LAURA DOVER is an editorial assistant for Lark Books. She lives in Asheville, North Carolina, where she enjoys free-lance writing and playing with her chocolate Labrador puppy, Emma.

SUSAN FORREST combines her lifelong interests of gardening and painting through her business, Great Gourds. She grows and cures all of her own gourds, then transforms them into richly detailed, one-of-a-kind Santas. She lives in Sturgeon, Missouri.

VICKI GADBERRY is an information specialist and fiber artist living in Marshall, North Carolina. Like all fiber lovers, she collects fabric remnants, which she enjoys quilting into a variety of decorative items.

LORRAINE GOUGE is a multimedia artist who has worked in papier-mâché for about 15 years. She trained in Norway and France and currently lives in Spruce Pine, North Carolina, where she exhibits her paintings and papier-mâché works in local galleries.

MARGARET (PEGGY) HAYES lives in Fletcher, North Carolina, where she creates custom cross-stitch designs. She especially enjoys designing graphs for clients to stitch pictures of their own homes, and she credits much of her inspiration to her husband of 24 years, Charles.

CHRISTI HENSLEY uses the kitchen of her home in Barnardsville, North Carolina, as a part-time studio for making a limited number of heirloom Santas and angels every year. Most of these are marketed through word of mouth, but she also displays her work in area craft shows.

DANA IRWIN, in addition to being an art director for Lark Books, likes to dance, make music, and create art. She lives in Asheville, North Carolina with her dog and two cats.

LORI KERR designs fabric jewelry and textile art pieces as well as clothing, but she most enjoys sharing her skills through teaching. She lives in Durham, North Carolina.

VIRGINIA KILLMORE is a full-time dollmaker and artist in Syracuse, New York. She manages her business, Virginia's American Folk Dolls, from her home studio. Her dolls are sold in specialty stores throughout the United States, and some have been displayed at the White House.

GUY KOPPI expresses his creativity through drawing and painting and frequently involves his wife and three children in his projects. A resident of Black Mountain, North Carolina, he has 20 years of experience as a printer and currently works with handicapped adults.

DIANE C. KUEBITZ, who lives in Sandy, Utah, draws her inspiration from whimsical spirits and numerous nature guides. Her six-year-old son, Edward, often helps her name the figures she creates from polymer clay.

ALICE M. LAWSON is a native of Western North Carolina who has been carving wood as a hobby for eight years. She specializes in Santas and likes to give most of them away to her five daughters and seven grandchildren.

CLAUDIA LEE is a full-time studio papermaker and instructor in Kingsport, Tennessee. All of her hand-made paper figures, which are sold through area shops and galleries, are invested with a large measure of good humor.

CONTRIBUTING DESIGNERS

FLETA MONAGHAN is a part-time bookkeeper in Asheville, North Carolina, but her real loves are creating mixed-media sculptures, drawing, and painting. Her daughter, Mary, provides lots of design ideas and likes to help make projects and show them at craft fairs.

MARY PARKER pursues a career in public sector finance in order to indulge her passion for fabric. She lives in Asheville, North Carolina, with her husband and six cats.

NAN AND BILL PARKER are teachers who retired from Florida to Mountain Rest, South Carolina. They enjoy crafting for friends and for craft shows.

CATHERINE REURS, a former career banker in Europe, is an internationally known needlepoint and cross-stitch designer. Her designs are featured in her book, *In Splendid Detail: Needlepoint Art*, and she sells her needlepoint and cross-stitch kits through her business, In Splendid Detail, in Watertown, Massachusetts.

BEVERLY ROBBINS is a self-taught artist who lives in the shadow of Mount Shasta in Northern California. Her love affair with gourds began in 1991, and when she's not painting cat Santas, she favors Northwestern and Southwestern designs.

CATHI ROSENGREN was a cosmetics executive for 15 years prior to opening her shop, i'm in stitches, in Newburyport, Massachusetts. In her classes, she shares her passion for needlepoint by combining fine, hand-painted canvases with her imaginative use of fibers and stitches.

MARY BETH RUBY, of Bellefonte, Pennsylvania, began sculpting as a child. Today she creates papier-mâché animals, figurines, bowls, and jewelry. She creates commissioned works and frequently exhibits her sculptures in one-person and juried shows.

MARY SAVAGE is a fiber artist who most enjoys needlework and creating soft sculpture. She lives in Monona, Wisconsin, where she works as a photo stylist and a prop artist.

PAT SCHEIBLE, a former research biologist, keeps busy with trompe l'oeil and faux finish work for commercial and residential clients in the southeast. Her highly creative ideas are applied to everything from painted furniture to custom clothing. She lives in Mebane, North Carolina.

GINGER SUMMIT is the owner of Summit Designs in Los Altos, California. Coauthor of *The Complete Book of Gourd Craft* (Lark Books, 1996), Ginger derives great pleasure from working with gourds and using them in her home.

GAY SYMMES is a Texas native who now lives in Asheville, North Carolina. Her needlework has earned awards from the Houston Contemporary Arts Museum and from state and county fairs. Her avocation grew into a cottage industry during the 1980s, when she supplied needlework to a Dallas mail-order house.

TERRY TAYLOR creates art for the garden using the pique-assiette technique for making mosaics. He also combines pique-assiette with tramp art carving to make decorative objects for interior spaces. He collects, creates, and carves from his home in Asheville, North Carolina.

KIM TIBBALS is an art director and graphic designer who pours much of her artistic energy into drawing, sewing, herbal crafts, gardening, and broom making. She lives in Waynesville, North Carolina.

DAVID VANCE is a seminary graduate and a self-taught artist who lives in Asheville, North Carolina. He began by carving people, angels, and animals from wood. Although he currently spends more time painting on canvas, he can't entirely put aside his carving.

MARY KAY WEST has been sewing since she was a child. She left a career as a clinical psychologist to design one-of-a-kind clothing and accessories. For the past 10 years, one of the hallmarks of her designs has been the creative use of stiffened fabrics. She lives in Asheville, North Carolina.

INDEX

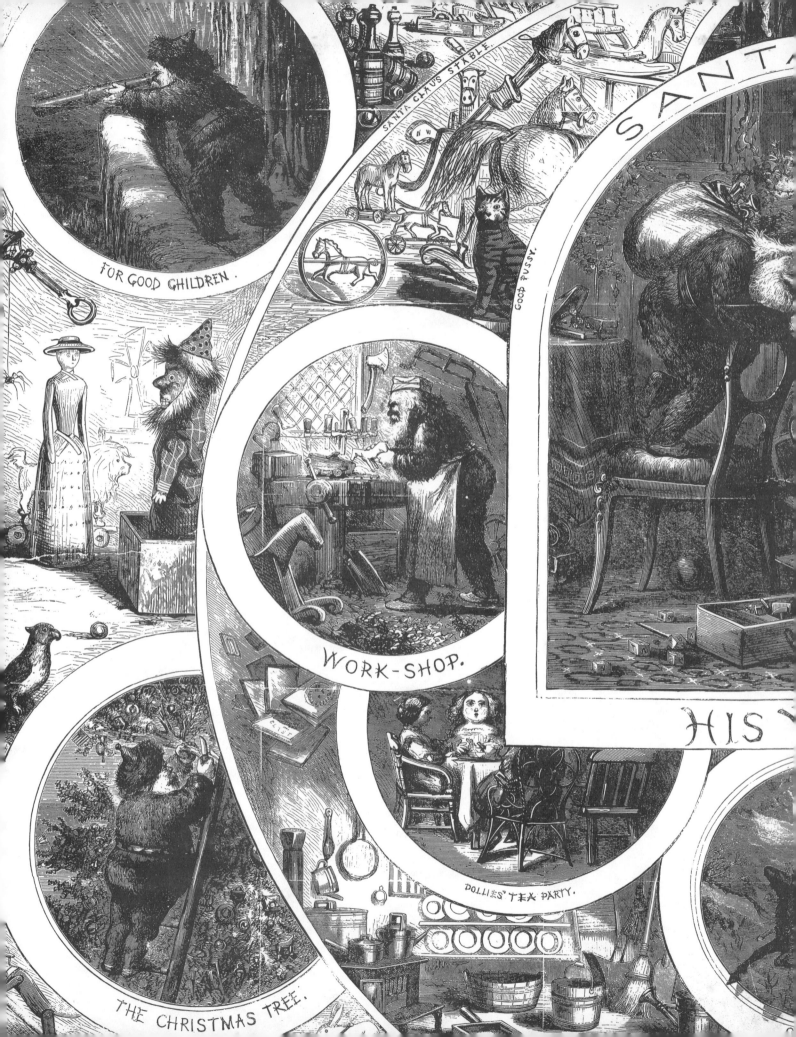

SANTA

HIS

FOR GOOD CHILDREN.

SANTA CLAUS STABLE.

GOOD PUSSY.

WORK-SHOP.

DOLLIES' TEA PARTY.

THE CHRISTMAS TREE.